Garland Studies in

THE HISTORY OF AMERICAN LABOR

edited by

STUART BRUCHEY
ALLAN NEVINS PROFESSOR EMERITUS
COLUMBIA UNIVERSITY

A GARLAND SERIES

UNCOVERING THE HIDDEN WORK OF WOMEN IN FAMILY BUSINESSES

A History of Census Undernumeration

LISA GEIB-GUNDERSON

GARLAND PUBLISHING, Inc.
A MEMBER OF THE TAYLOR & FRANCIS GROUP
NEW YORK & LONDON / 1998

Library of Congress Cataloging-in-Publication Data

Geib-Gunderson, Lisa, 1967–
    Uncovering the hidden work of women in family businesses :
a history of census undernumeration / Lisa Geib-Gunderson.
        p.   cm. — (Garland studies in the history of American
labor)
    Includes bibliographical references and index.
    ISBN 0-8153-3253-X (alk. paper)
    1. Women—Employment—United States—History.
2. Family-owned business enterprises—United States—Employees—History. 3. Census undercounts—United States—History.
4. United States—Census—History. I. Title. II. Series.
HD6095.G44 1998
331.4'0973—dc21

                                                    98-46218

Printed on acid-free, 250-year-life paper
Manufactured in the United States of America

For Craig,
without whom this would not exist

Contents

Tables and Figures

Acknowledgments

Thanks are due Susan Carter for her many hours of guidance and motivation. Her unfailingly high expectations often made me feel like giving up, but in the end made me a better economist. I also thank Dave Fairris for providing insightful suggestions that improved my work tremendously. In addition, I owe a debt of gratitude, which I may never be able to repay, to my family for the sacrifices they made while I produced this book.

Most of all I thank my husband, Craig Gundersen, who has taught me more during the past six years than I had learned in my entire life before.

Uncovering the Hidden Work of Women in Family Businesses

The popular impression seems to be that women today are taking a larger share of the world's work than they have ever done before—that this is a new departure, the outcome of the factory system. As a matter of fact the share taken by women in the work of the world has not altered in amount, or even in intensity, only in character. Even in character it has not changed as much as the working man imagines.

Ada Heather-Bigg, 1894

CHAPTER I

An Historical Description of Married Women's Labor

THE U-SHAPED PATTERN OF MARRIED WOMEN'S LABOR SUPPLY

Data from the United States Census of Population indicate that there has been a dramatic increase in the labor force participation of married women over the twentieth century. This book takes issue with this well-known stylized fact.

Census figures indicate that in 1900 the labor force participation rate of married women was 5.3 percent and that by 1990 this rate had climbed to 57.7 percent (see Table 1.1).[1] Virtually all studies of early female labor force participation in the U.S. are based upon the census, which first collected data on women's occupations in 1860, first collected this data by marital status in 1880, and first published aggregate statistics of marital status and occupation in 1890.[2] Extrapolation to earlier years is based upon our knowledge of production practices in the colonial period of the United States. Married women's participation is thought to have followed a pronounced U-shaped pattern, first falling and then rising with industrialization.[3]

Claudia Goldin (1994) explains that the basis for this pattern rests in our understanding that in the colonial period, household production was the dominant form of market activity with married women playing key roles in household production. Therefore, during these early years, women's participation rates were very high. The left-hand, or declining phase of the U is said to have resulted from the separation of home from work in the early stages of industrialization (between the colonial period and the early twentieth century). In this phase, men are said to have followed "work" out of the home while their wives remained in the home, specializing in the production of goods and services for the consumption of their families. Since this household production is not generally defined as "work", married women's employment rates fell. The right-hand, or increasing phase of the U is said to represent a new era in which educated married women, after World War II, increasingly found employment opportunities in while collar occupations outside the home.

Whereas the labor force literature comments extensively on men's transition from home production to market work, the effect on women's employment has gone more or less unnoticed. We know from labor force statistics that this structural shift was accompanied by a decline in the proportion of men who were self-employed and an increase in the number who work for wages or salaries. However, the effect of such structural shifts on women's economic activity is not completely clear since, for the most part, the United States labor force statistics do not report their participation as *unpaid family workers*.[4] As women shifted from unpaid family labor to more easily recognizable wage work, the labor force statistics reported an increase in the general rate of participation. It *appears*, therefore, women's increased labor force participation was brought about by industrialization.

There have been numerous feminist critiques of this conventional belief which have as their premise a challenge to the categorization of the unpaid household production of married women as something other than "work".[5] According to this view, the amount of work performed by married women did not change over the course of industrialization but, rather, the location of their work activity changed—especially relative to that of men.

The starting point of this book is fundamentally different. I accept, for example, the standard definition of "work" as involvement in GNP-producing activity. Instead, I focus on the timing and extent of the decline in the family economy (or the unity of home and work) that facilitated the productive employment of married women prior to industrialization. Census data indicate that self-employment was chosen by families in the American economy well into the twentieth century. This institution, therefore, remained a viable one for women's participation in GNP-producing activities far longer than is generally recognized.[6] The objective of this book is to uncover the work usually omitted from descriptions of wage work and housework—that is, work done in the household for market use—and to examine the various implications of this omission for analyzing married women's participation in GNP-producing work over the course of the past century. In so doing, I find levels and trends in participation that are significantly different from the standard view.

FROM HOUSEHOLD PRODUCTION TO LABOR MARKET PARTICIPATION

Work performed by both men and women can be categorized into two basic types: work involved in the production of goods and services to be sold in the market (GNP type) and work involved in the production of goods and services to be consumed directly (non-GNP type). Both types of work are necessary in any economy and both can be performed at home or outside the home. Below I reproduce a chart devised by Penelope Ciancanelli (1983) which categorizes this labor by the *location of production* (home/outside the home) and the *destination of outputs* (market/own use).[7]

Figure 1.1: The Locational and Destination Dimensions of Women's Work

	For Market	*For Own Use*
At Home	Farm wives harvesting cash crop Taking in boarders and lodgers Piece work for local factory	Repairing and improving home Cooking and cleaning Child care
Outside the Home	Wage work in office/factory Peddling, selling Running a business outside home	Subsistence farming

These locational and destination dimensions of work are of particular interest in the study of women's economic activity during the early decades of this century. While in the current period in the United States most home production is for own use and most "outside the home" production is for market, this was not always the case. In the years around the turn of the century and before, many women produced market goods at home. However, this does not mean that their work was entirely devoted to the production of use values for the consumption of their families.

The "social relationship" of labor is analyzed by Ciancanelli using Census-related terms describing work relations. This analysis is characterized in Chart 2 below.[8] The point of this chart is that, although both unpaid family labor (production of goods and services within the home for sale in the market) and wage work are *market* work, they are fundamentally different in terms of institutional and societal ideology. The implications of these differences for counting women's work are discussed in the next section.

Figure 1.2: The Social Relations of Production

	Social Relations			
	Unpaid Family Worker	*Self-Employed*	*Employee*	*Employer*
Own Use	Housework	Subsistence farming		Supervising servants
Market	Farm wives Small business	Farmer, Artisan Boarding services Taking in laundry	Wage worker	Running a small business with hired help

EARLY CENSUS BIASES

In this book, I argue that married women were, in fact, participating in the labor market through their activities in family businesses much later in the twentieth century than is generally recognized. A close examination of Census enumerator instructions reveals a number of factors that led to the exclusion of many married women from official employment statistics in the earliest years of data collection (1880 through 1930).[9] The census office itself recognized this problem and the possibility of enumerator error was openly acknowledged:

> Women and children are omitted in large numbers . . . either through failure of the enumerator to ask the questions related to occupation concerning such persons, assuming that they have no avocation outside their homes, or from the indisposition of the persons themselves or the heads of families to speak of them as in employment.[10]

There is reason to doubt the standard U-shaped story and, in particular, the low rates of participation recorded for married women (the bottom of the "U") around the turn of the century. Understanding the factors that led to this omission makes this fact clear; these are discussed below.

Changes in definition: The recorded level of married women's participation may have been too low in the earliest years of the census due to the manner in which a person's employment status was recorded by enumerators. The technical definition of employment has changed since 1880, becoming more inclusive of women's work since 1940. Prior to 1940, a person was recorded as "gainfully occupied" if he or she (but usually he) reported having an occupation, whether or not the person was currently working, retired, or working only seasonally.[11] The social identification with one's occupation meant that if a person thought of himself as a cranberry bog laborer because it was what he had spent his life doing (even if he hadn't bogged cranberries for a number of years) he could classify himself as having such an occupation simply by responding appropriately.

The situation changed in 1940 when, as a result of the New Deal's attempt to gain a more accurate picture of the unemployment situation following the Great Depression, the modern labor force concept was adopted. Respondents were asked specifically about the previous week's activity, rather than open-ended questions about occupation. The well-known criteria for being classified as a member of the labor force was that the person must have been working for wages or actively looking for work for at least one hour during the previous week, or working regularly[12] at unpaid family labor (such as working on family farms or businesses, and providing services for boarders) for at least fifteen hours during the previous week.[13] A woman might in 1880, therefore, report herself as a housewife while performing substantial work on her family's farm and end up not being classified as gainfully occupied due to her reported occupation. On the other hand, the same woman in 1940 would have been classified as gainfully occupied when enumerators asked about her activities rather than occupations (provided she did this farm work for more than fourteen hours each week). For this reason, women's recorded participation rates prior to 1940 are probably underestimates of their true market work.

Respondent Bias: A second reason to question census labor force statistics is that respondents are allowed only one occupation to be recorded in the census[14]. To avoid the stigma that was attached to women who relinquished their roles as housewives during the "cult of domesticity" of this period, women would often give "keeping house" as their primary activity even if they did other work for pay such as cooking and cleaning for boarders, factory home work, taking in laundry, or nonpaying family work such as working on farms.[15] In Francis Amasa Walker's[16] words, "ladies themselves are reluctant to acknowledge that they worked for a living".[17]

Enumerator Bias: As mentioned in the beginning of this section, a significant factor in the undercount of productive women was that census enumerators themselves sometimes simply assumed that women were not employed without even asking. Again, Walker says, the "assumption is ... that they are not engaged in remunerative employments. [A]ssistant marshals will not infrequently forget or neglect to ask the question".[18] Perhaps the assistant marshals "forgot" or "neglected" to ask about women's occupations after having read Walker's statement on women that "we may assume that speaking broadly, she does not produce as much as she consumes".[19] In any event, the resulting census publications failed to report many women who worked part-time or in unpaid family businesses as gainfully occupied, whereas economically inactive men might theoretically have been counted as fully employed for the reasons outlined in the previous section.

Procedural Bias: The perceived increase in the female labor force participation rate was further solidified by the changing occupational structure which brought many women into more visible jobs outside their homes in clerical, service, and manufacturing positions. At the turn of the century, family farms and businesses played a crucial role in the American economy. Many women who were employed at home doing "hidden" work in these enterprises were overlooked by census enumerators. The quantitative importance of the gender bias inherent in the census data began to decrease as the percentage of self-employed and agricultural households decreased over the century. Issues of consistency and bias, then, are most problematic in the earliest years of the census.

Each of the above sources of bias demonstrate, if nothing else, that the concept of unpaid family labor was very much subject to societal assumptions that led to the gender discrepancies in the early censuses. After all, why should "family employment" be treated different from "self-employment"? Unpaid family labor does *not* include housework or childcare but is restricted to work performed as part of a family business enterprise. The primary difference between the self-employed, defined as labor force participants after one hour of work, and the family-employed, considered labor force participants only after fifteen hours, is that the former were primarily adult married males, and the latter were overwhelmingly women and children.[20] The self-employed were often quite dependent upon family labor, and the distinction between them and unpaid family workers is highly arbitrary.

THE IMPORTANCE OF COUNTING WOMEN'S WORK

Claudia Goldin argues that of all historical change in the female labor force, the increased participation of married women has been the most meaningful. It has been associated with a decline in the stability of the family, with altered gender relations, and with an increase in the political power of women. The shift of married women's work from production for direct use to production for the market has been accompanied by social and political change of enormous consequence.[21] *Why* their employment increased is the subject of Goldin's book, *Understanding the Gender Gap* (1990). *Whether* their employment increased is the subject of this book.

In a review of Goldin (1990), Gavin Wright suggests that her analysis of the female labor force participation rate over the past century, particularly that of married women, provides insight into the deep question: "Are the trends in women's work and pay governed by "market fundamentals," or are they instead a reflection of changes in attitudes, institutions, political power, and other apparently noneconomic factors?"[22] Goldin's focus in answering this question is on the change in the relative gender wage gap over the course of the century that brought many married women into the paid labor force and she, therefore, concentrates on *wage* labor. While both Goldin and Wright are concerned with the nature and change of women's work, in this book I focus on the relationship between married women and home production for the market (unpaid family labor that contributes to GNP) and the extent to which this work has been undercounted, precisely because of "changes in attitudes, institutions, political power, and other apparently noneconomic factors."

In addition to the question posed by Wright, a thorough examination of census biases may shed light on many other unresolved problems in the literature. One such issue is the degree of accuracy in estimates of U.S. productivity growth over the twentieth century. Geib-Gundersen and Zahrt (1996) find that because a large number of farm laborers were erroneously calculated as nonfarm laborers by the Census Bureau in 1880 and 1900, previous estimates of agricultural productivity (farm output per worker) were too high (and hence, previous estimates of industrial productivity were too low). Geib-Gundersen and Zahrt did not, however, consider the effects of the undercounting of unpaid family farm workers. Including all married women who performed GNP-type work on family farms from 1880 to 1900 would increase the size of the agricultural work force even more dramatically than Geib-Gundersen and Zahrt's estimates. Thus, agricultural productivity over this period may indeed have been even *lower* than their already lower estimates.

The effect of women's participation on the U.S. economy was not, however, restricted to the agricultural sector. The transition by married women from home production (of the GNP-type) to the wage labor force most likely affected the very institution of self-employment. Carter and Sutch (1996) ask the question: why has self-employment declined so dramatically over the course of the twentieth century? One answer may lie in the "hidden" work of married women in family businesses. As opportunities increased in the wage labor force for such women, many were induced to leave their careers in family enterprises for the high-paying jobs outside the home. Perhaps it was the case that these women played such crucial roles in the operation of family businesses that their entry into paid labor resulted in the demise of the profitability of self-employment for many families.

Prior to this demise, however, we know that the rate of self-employment among married men varied dramatically by race [Fairlie (1996) and Fairlie and Meyer (1996)]. Because of this fact, an examination of women's underenumeration can provide explanations for the apparent gap in the labor force participation between black and white married women. A vast literature has been devoted to understanding the fact that, even when controlling for differences in family income and unemployment, black married women appear to have supplied abundantly more labor to the market than their white counterparts.[23] In this book, I argue that the primary reason for our previous inability to explain over 30 percent of this adjusted gap is the reliance on census occupation statistics which underestimate the contributions of women's work in family businesses. Indeed, if it is the case that women were underreported in occupation statistics and if it can be shown that this underreporting itself differed by race, then we may gain insight into the nature of what Goldin (1977) refers to as "the social stigmatization of work" experienced largely by white, married women around the turn of the century that, she claims, has been resistant to change and lingered for many years.

The format of this book is as follows. Chapter II presentd a summary of the issues on the undercount of women workers as it has been posed in the historical literature on women and work in the United States from 1880 to 1940. It also introduces the data set employed in this book, the Public Use Microdata Sample (PUMS).

This lays the groundwork for Chapter III in which a detailed characterization of women's uncounted work in family businesses is presented. This analysis compiles descriptive statistics on the nature of turn-of-the-century self-employment, provides a review of documentary evidence on the activities of the wives with self-employed husbands, and estimates the extent of women's involvement in such ventures.

The results from Chapter III are decomposed by race in Chapter IV in which a theoretical model of married women's labor supply is presented which departs from the well-known Mincer-type models in that it includes information on the husband's "class of worker" status (whether the husband worked for wages or was self-employed). By incorporating this new aspect of the determination of women's contributions to GNP-type activities, I am able to offer a cogent explanation for the previously unexplainable portion of the racial gap in married women's labor force participation.

Finally, in Chapter V, the evidence developed in the preceding chapters is brought together, implications are discussed, and suggestions are made for further research.

Table 1.1: Female Labor Force Participation By Race, Marital Status, and Age, 1880-1940

Age	Single		Married		All Marital Groups	
	Black	*White*	*Black*	*White*	*Black*	*White*
1880						
15-19	59.9	26.2	34.7	2.3	56.2	23.7
20-29	71.3	40.6	30.5	1.8	46.4	18.0
30-39	73.5	40.3	28.5	1.9	41.5	9.6
40-49	76.8	34.9	24.7	1.7	39.4	8.4
50-64	64.7	28.2	24.4	1.2	38.6	7.3
over 64	36.5	8.8	18.8	0.9	23.4	4.4
All ages	65.2	32.8	28.2	1.7	44.0	13.6
1900						
15-19	51.9	30.4	23.3	3.1	48.5	27.6
20-29	75.7	55.2	22.9	1.5	44.6	25.8
30-39	78.6	56.3	25.6	2.6	43.6	14.8
40-49	75.0	45.4	21.0	2.8	42.8	13.0
50-64	61.5	40.7	22.0	2.4	44.0	14.0
over 64	50.0	18.0	18.0	1.6	27.2	8.6
All ages	66.5	41.0	22.1	2.3	41.8	17.3

Table 1.1: Female Labor Force Participation By Race, Marital Status, and Age, 1880-1940 (continued)

Age	Single Black	Single White	Married Black	Married White	All Marital Groups Black	All Marital Groups White
1910						
15-19	65.0	35.5	52.5	7.0	63.0	32.5
20-29	82.5	63.2	53.0	6.4	63.7	29.6
30-39	88.9	65.2	51.4	6.6	61.4	18.3
40-49	91.1	58.5	50.2	7.1	62.2	17.2
50-64	75.0	44.4	50.6	5.2	60.6	13.7
over 64	50.0	16.2	30.0	2.8	34.4	6.7
All ages	73.4	49.6	51.3	6.3	61.2	21.9
1940						
15-19	32.1	23.3	19.6	7.7	31.8	21.9
20-29	71.5	77.3	27.6	17.4	47.2	41.4
30-39	74.2	77.6	26.9	15.6	44.2	27.3
40-49	65.9	68.7	23.1	11.4	38.7	22.1
50-64	47.6	53.1	19.6	6.9	31.8	16.7
over 64	35.7	18.8	9.2	2.5	12.7	5.9
All ages	49.8	50.1	24.6	12.4	38.7	25.0

Married includes married, spouse present and married, spouse absent in 1880, 1990, and 1910. It includes married, spouse present in 1940, 1980, and 1990. Single includes single and unknown in 1880, 1900, and 1910. It includes single only in 1940, 1980, and 1990.

As reported by census enumerators, the figures for 1910 are not directly comparable with the other years due to the well-documented "overcount" of agricultural workers, particularly women, in this year. See Chapter II for a discussion.

Source for All Tables: Public Use Microdata Samples (1880 through 1990), unless otherwise noted.

NOTES

1. Prior to 1940 the "gainful worker" concept of employment was used by the census rather than the "labor force" concept we use today. Individuals were counted in the labor force under the gainful worker concept if they claimed to have had an occupation during the census year. By contrast, individuals are counted in the labor force under the modern labor force concept if they worked for wages during the previous week at least one hour, worked in a family business at least fifteen hours, or were unemployed but actively looked for work. Goldin (1986) argues that because of a number of different offsetting factors, there is no reason why one definition should result in a higher value than the other. I use the term "labor force participation" throughout this paper to refer to participation in the labor market under either the gainful worker or labor force concept. Also see Geib-Gundersen (1995) and Bancroft (1958), Appendix C, for a discussion of the differences between and consistency in the two measures.

2. Abel and Folbre (1990), p. 167.

3. Goldin (1994).

4. U.S. Censuses (1880 through 1930). Unpaid family labor, as defined by the Census Bureau, does *not* include housework or childcare, but is restricted to work performed as a part of a family business enterprise.

5. See Folbre (1991) for a review.

6. Carter and Sutch (1996).

7. Ciancanelli (1983) p. 38.

8. Ciancanelli (1983), p. 38.

9. See below for a discussion of the change in the census of 1940 that made the count of gainful workers more inclusive of women's work after that year.

10. U.S. Census (1883), p. x.

11. Abel and Folbre (1990), p. 169.

12. A requirement never imposed on men.

13. U.S. Census (1883), Instructions to Enumerators.

14. Historically women have been more likely than men to combine market work with work in the home. To make them choose one occupation over the other understates the extent of women's contributions.

15. Carroll Wright reflected the spirit of the cult of domesticity when writing in a special report on the 1880 census that "the employment of married women, it seems to me, is the very worst feature of factory employment"

(quoted in Abel and Folbre 1990).

16. Superintendent of the 1880 Census.
17. Quoted in Folbre (1991).
18. Folbre (1991).
19. Walker (1883).
20. U.S. Censuses (1880 through 1940).
21. Goldin (1990).
22. Wright (1991), p. 1153.
23. See Goldin (1977), Bowen and Finegan (1969), Cain (1966), and Bell (1974). This issue is addressed fully in Chapter 4.

CHAPTER II

The Apparent Undercount of Productive Women in the United States

Recall the U-shaped pattern of married women's GNP-producing work described in Chapter I. The theory behind this pattern relies on the fact that in the earliest years of U.S. history, family production for the market implied high work rates for married women since they were crucial members of the family production unit that dominated the nation's economy at that time. For consistency with this theory, estimates of the number of gainfully occupied women in later years must also capture such women. A close examination of census data, however, indicates that the majority of women with self-employed husbands were excluded from employment statistics before 1940.

In censuses before 1940, a respondent was counted as gainfully occupied if he or she reported having an occupation. Beginning in 1940, the current definition of labor force participation was adopted and respondents were counted as gainfully occupied if they reported having worked for wages for at least one hour during the previous week, working as an unpaid family worker for at least fifteen hours, or actively looking for employment during the previous week.[1] The "cult of domesticity" discussed in Chapter I that made married women hesitant to identify themselves as having any occupation other than housewife suggests that the pre-1940 definition of gainful occupation was linked to social identity rather than economic activity. Measured labor force participation, therefore, is more inclusive of women's work after 1940. This definitional change is most likely responsible for much of the measured increase in the participation rates of married women after 1940 (see Table 1.1 in Chapter I).

More specifically, there are two factors which suggest that the undercount of married women working in family businesses was significantly smaller in 1940 and later years. The first is the shift from the gainful worker to the labor force concept discussed above. The second is the declining rate of self-employment that left significantly fewer women with self-employed husbands (see Table 3.1 in Chapter III). Therefore, since the enumeration of women was most problematic in the earliest years of the census (and is, in fact, taken to be accurate by most scholars in the 1940 and later data), the analysis in this chapter will focus on 1880 through 1910.[2]

A vast literature has been devoted to analyzing the extent of underenumeration in early labor force statistics.[3] Missing from this literature, however, is a detailed study of women's role in family businesses. The goal of this chapter and the next is to demonstrate that women's unpaid labor in family businesses was the main source of underenumeration in the early censuses. Understanding women's role in the institution of self-employment is the key to answering many questions about their work history that have previously remained ambiguous.

To facilitate this understanding, I begin with a brief discussion of women's enumeration in the earliest years of the census (1880 through 1930). I then review the literature on the claim that the enumeration in these years represented a significant undercount of women performing GNP-type work and discuss the four major methods of proposed adjustment, pointing to the limitations of each.[4] Next, I introduce the data set to be used in this and subsequent chapters, the Public Use Microdata Sample (PUMS), and employ this data to make some preliminary, upper-bound adjustments to the labor force participation rates of married women. These adjustments demonstrate the significance of women's role in self-employment. I discuss the framework for analyzing this role in more detail in Chapter III.

WOMEN IN EARLY CENSUSES

Perhaps it is not surprising that so many married women may have been excluded from the early censuses. The first census of the United States was conducted in 1790 and asked questions of families only. The first inquiry on individuals' occupations within families was the 1850 census, but this data was collected solely for males. Finally, in 1860 data was collected on women's occupations and, in 1880, it was collected by marital status.[5]

Posed in this light, it may seem surprising that as *early* as 1910, the Census Bureau recognized the problem of possible undercounting and explicitly instructed its enumerators to consider the occupations of married women: "The occupation, if any, followed by a child, of any age, or by a woman is just as important, for census purposes, as the occupation followed by a man. Therefore it must never be taken for granted, without inquiry, that a woman or child has no occupation".[6] The resulting published figures for this year displayed a dramatic increase in the number of women reporting an occupation. However, instead of prompting a reconsideration of previous years' estimates, 1910 was seen as a discontinuity and the above wording was dropped from the 1920 instructions to enumerators, resulting in a drop in the percentage of married women classified as gainfully occupied in this year. Most later literature on labor force statistics treated it as an anomaly.[7]

Many economists considered the 1910 estimates to be the most reliable and have inspired much research on the subject. From this research has emerged the point of view that even the 1910 estimates, in fact, still represent an undercount of working women.

A REVIEW OF THE CENSUS UNDERCOUNT LITERATURE

A. J. Jaffe (1956) was the first modern labor economist to question the reliability of the reported increase in women's labor force participation from 1880 to 1950. He argued three propositions: (a) that the gainful worker series undercounted working women relative to the modern series because of its treatment of part-time, seasonal, and self-employed workers; (b) that the reported increase in women's labor force participation did not reflect the true increase in their work rates but changes in Census procedures over time; and (c) that the 1910 estimates were the most reliable of the pre-1940 censuses. He concluded therefore that the 1880 to 1930 trend given by the gainful worker data for women was unreliable. *If* their long-term labor force participation could be reliably estimated, he argued, it would show little and possibly no increase over that period. Although Jaffe clearly indicated his belief that women in self-employed households were undercounted, no subsequent study has paid much attention to such women.

In 1959 and 1960, Robert Smuts offered even more extensive criticisms of the early census returns and proposed that the pre-1910 censuses considerably underreported the number of women engaged in farm labor. After these major critiques, however, the issue was not to be raised again, nor addressed by the Census Bureau, for a number of years. The recent efforts to revitalize the underenumeration issue have been sparked primarily by economists seeking to provide post-enumeration adjustments to the published labor force statistics on women in order to gain a more accurate picture of their work history. All four of the major efforts to revise the labor force series argue that women's contributions to the economy have been substantially undercounted. Their findings and motivations, however, differ widely. These four adjustment methods are now described.

The research of Penelope Ciancanelli (1983), Christine Bose (1987), Claudia Goldin (1989), and Marjorie Abel and Nancy Folbre (1990) suggests that the causes of the perceived increase in the female labor force participation rate since 1880 are directly related to those discussed in Chapter I, namely (a) the change in the Census Office's approach to counting GNP-type work and (b) the shift in female employment from domestic and farm activities to work outside the home where it is more easily identified and counted.

Ciancanelli bases her revisions on early Women's Bureau[8] studies and suggests that married women's labor force participation for 1900 to 1930 was ten times higher than the census estimates. Bose uses the 1900 Public Use Sample to propose a similar increase. Goldin's revisions, based upon a number of sources, suggest a tripling of the married women's labor force participation rate for 1890. Finally, Abel and Folbre use the federal manufacturing census and the Massachusetts state census of 1875 to find upward revisions in participation of over four times in two New England towns.[9]

Goldin's study is primarily concerned with achieving consistency between the pre- and post-1940 definitions of employment. Bose, Ciancanelli, and Abel and Folbre are more concerned with correcting the census' gender bias in the early years. They claim that since any participation in the market qualified males as labor force participants before 1940, the same should hold for women.[10]

As a group, these authors concentrate on three areas in which women's work has been undercounted. These areas include (a) women providing boarding services such as cooking, cleaning, and laundering, (b) women farmers and farm laborers working without pay on family farms and, to less of an extent, (c) women in self-employed households assisting with family businesses. The methods and findings of each study are examined in turn under these three areas of potential undercount.

BOARDERS

Women who lived in households that took in boarders provided cooking, cleaning, and laundering services. Ciancanelli's approach to adjusting the undercount of women providing boarding services is to generalize for the period 1900 to 1920 the fact that in 1920, 30% of all married women lived in households which took in boarders. She assumes that all of these women met the requisite fifteen hour per week minimum and thus includes them all in the count of gainfully occupied women.

Bose finds for 1900 that 10% of females between the ages of 15-64 lived in households with boarders. Since single women in households with boarders had a recorded participation rate of over 40 percent while wives in such households reported only 5.4 percent, she argues that census enumerators overlooked the work of married women and adds them all to the labor force, thereby increasing their participation rate by 3.4 percentage points.

Goldin finds that in 1890, 16 percent of families with husbands and wives in cities of 25,000 or more took in boarders. She assumes that providing services to boarders involved at least fifteen hours of unpaid family labor from married women and, thus, includes all of these wives in the count of gainful workers.

Abel and Folbre find that in 1880, 21.8 percent of all women over the age of fifteen lived in households with boarders in the towns they analyzed. They also assumed that these women worked for the boarders for at least fifteen hours per week and added them all to the labor force. Clearly, a credible reestimation of this aspect of women's work requires more information on the contribution of other family members in the household, the labor requirements per boarder, and the average number of boarders per household in each year.

FARMS

On adjusting the count of women working on farms from 1900 to 1930, Ciancanelli uses the 1910 census estimate of women employed on farms as a lower-bound under the assumption that farm wives probably participated in even more farm work in earlier years. As an upper-bound, she assumes that all farm wives worked at least fifteen hours per week in each year.

Bose examines the number of servants and hired hands on farms (and off-farm employees) and proposes that the 96.5 percent of women in households with no servants or employees probably worked as farm laborers at least fifteen hours per week and should be included among the count of gainful workers in 1900.

Goldin, on the opposite side of Ciancanelli, uses the 1910 census estimates of unpaid family farm labor as an upper-bound. She argues that only major cotton-producing states suffered any significant undercount of women farm workers and estimates that such women worked an average of ten hours per week, or 20 percent of the average work week, and therefore adds 20 percent of farm wives living on non-cotton farms to the 1890 labor force count.[11]

Abel and Folbre assume that farm wives were just as likely to contribute to farm production for the market as their husbands. Therefore, they added all wives who had husbands who were farmers, but had no occupation listed for themselves and did not live in a household that took in boarders.

SELF-EMPLOYMENT

The institution of self-employment has received relatively little attention in the underenumeration literature. Goldin does not address the issue of women in self-employed households (with the exception of self-employed farmers, as discussed in the previous section). Ciancanelli suggests that since 21.2 percent of all wives of self-employed men were listed as gainfully occupied in a 1948 survey from the Women's Bureau, approximately the same number should be added to the labor force count for 1900 to 1930.

Bose simply assumes that half of such wives should be counted. Abel and Folbre use the same logic as they employed for farm wives to assume that any married woman was just as likely to perform market work as her self-employed husband and accordingly add all such wives to the labor force. These estimates are clearly very ad hoc and would be more convincing if they controlled for differences in household income and examined the extent of women's participation in family businesses by occupation in each year. These issues are addressed in the next section and, in more detail, in Chapters III and IV.

THE PUBLIC USE MICRODATA SAMPLE (PUMS)

These studies have provided us with the foundation upon which to examine women's participation around the turn of the century. Unfortunately they had to rely on *published* census data which was often altered by the Census Bureau prior to its release.[12] With the recent release of the Public Use Microdata Sample (PUMS) for 1880, 1900, and 1910, we now have the opportunity to examine the issues raised in the previous section more reliably than ever before.[13] The individual-level data contained in the PUMS has made available a wealth of opportunities for exciting research, not the least of which is an examination of the occupational status of married women. The PUMS was produced by the Social Science Research Laboratory at the University of Minnesota and for 1880 is a 1-in-100 sample, for 1900 is a 1-in-760 sample, and for 1910 is a 1-in-250 sample of original census enumeration forms. Data on women contained in the PUMS for these years consist of a nationally-representative sample of 180,396 female observations in 1880; 36,938 in 1900; and 135,315 in 1910. The PUMS records information *as reported by census enumerators* and, therefore, does not reflect the post-enumeration editing by the Census Bureau.[14]

The extent of such editing can be observed in Tables 2.1 through 2.3 which list the population and occupational status of females, age 10 and over, as reported in the published census and the PUMS for each year. An examination of the ratio of PUMS to published data reveals that in 1880, the Census Bureau underreported women with occupations relative to the enumerator returns. In 1900, the extent of underreporting was somewhat less, and in 1910, the published data is nearly the same as the enumerator returns. These tables indicate that most of the underreporting of women workers, if it in fact existed on a large scale, appears to have been the cause of enumerator neglect rather than the post-enumeration editing at the Census Office.

The labor force attachment of married women was no doubt dependent upon many factors: her family's wealth and income, the geographical region in which she resided, her family size, whether she lived in an urban area or on a farm, whether she was in school, her age, race, and nativity,whether her household took in boarders,and whether her husband was self-employed.These variables,along with many more, are available in the PUMS and will be utilized extensively in this book.

WOMEN IN FAMILY BUSINESSES AND HOUSEHOLDS WITH BOARDERS

As discussed in the first section, consistency with the U-shaped pattern of married women's labor supply requires that estimates of the number of gainfully-occupied women include women working in family businesses. Furthermore, as suggested by the studies reviewed in the previous section, a large percentage of women who lived in households containing boarders should be included. An examination of the PUMS allows me to determine the number of such women who were *not* recorded as gainful workers in the relevant censuses.

Table 2.4 gives the percentages of married women living in households with self-employed men (farm and non-farm) or boarders, but not recorded as gainful workers in the census returns. Surprisingly, fully 57.2 percent of all married women had husbands who were self-employed in 1880 but were *not* recorded as gainfully occupied and an additional 3.3 percent of married women were living in households with boarders, but not counted as employed. In 1900, the percentages are 44.8 for self-employed and 5.6 for boarder households and for 1910, the percentages are 25.6 and 6.7, respectively.

To provide upper-bound estimates of the labor force participation rate of married women in each of these years that are consistent with the traditional U-shaped explanation of women's labor force pattern (as well as with Abel and Folbre's analysis), I add *all* of the women in these households to labor force. The revised labor force participation rates presented in Table 2.5 emerge and substantial increases are evident. The revised estimates obtained in this initial exercise are compared with the labor force participation rates of married women as reported in the PUMS and the published census in Table 2.6. As can be seen, these new estimates indicate that a substantial number of potentially gainfully occupied, married women were left out of the labor force estimates by both enumerators and editors of the published censuses. The inclusion of these women in self-employed and boarder households dramatically increases the labor force participation rate of married women from 4.6 to 65.1 percent in 1880, from 5.6 to 56.0 percent in 1900, and from 10.7 to 43.0 percent in 1910.

A second look at Table 1.1, combined with these upper-bound estimates for the years around the turn of the century, indicates that the implication of the revisions for the U-shaped explanation of the female labor force is that the more accurate pattern may be one of relative constancy across the century, marked by high participation rates in 1880, 1900, and 1910 (the traditional bottom of the "U"), a subsequent decline in 1940 as self-employment became less common, and a more gradual increase in participation after 1940, lasting through the current period. This revised pattern and its implications discussed in more detail in Chapter III.

AN ANALYSIS OF WOMEN'S INVOLVEMENT IN FAMILY BUSINESSES

The revisions suggested in the previous section, while made with more reliable data than has been available in the past, give us only a rough estimate of the number of women who participated in the labor market from 1880 to 1910. The claim of Abel and Folbre that *all* wives of self-employed men and Bose's claim that *all* farm wives should be added to the labor force can be strengthened by a more careful analysis of women's involvement, as Goldin provides in her analysis of women on farms and in boarder households. By extending Goldin's method of inquiry to women's activities in self-employment, examining a longer time period (1880 to 1990), and utilizing the more accurate PUMS data set to study the nature of self-employment-intensive occupations, I propose that we can gain significant insight into the extent to which women actually participated in their family's business. It is important to focus on this aspect of participation since, as was shown in the previous section, women's involvement in farm and non-farm self-employment seems to constitute the majority of the left-out labor (far greater than the excluded labor of providing boarding services).

We may find that Bose and Abel and Folbre are correct and that indeed, virtually all wives of self-employed men (farm and non-farm) participated in their family's business operations by staffing stores, keeping books, and even producing output. However, to assign a 100 percent probability of women's involvement a priori is not convincing.

In Chapter III, I examine thoroughly the nature of self-employment and self-employment-intensive occupations in order to offer more accurate probabilities of women's involvement in family businesses by type of occupation. With these estimates, new adjustments are made to the labor force statistics on married women and implications are discussed for the U-shaped pattern of participation over the course of the century.

Table 2.1: Occupational Status of Females, 1880 Published Census Totals and the Public Use Microdata Sample (PUMS)

Age	10 to 15	16 to 59	60 and Older	Total
	Published Census			
Population, 10 and Older	3,273,369	13,377,002	1,375,256	18,025,627
Recorded with Occupation	293,169	2,283,115	70,873	2,647,157
Recorded with no Occupation	2,980,200	11,093,887	1,304,383	15,378,470
	Public Use Microdata Sample (PUMS*100)			
Population, 10 and Older	3,275,500	13,371,200	1,392,900	18,039,600
Recorded with Occupation	395,800	3,287,700	174,300	3,838,400
Recorded with no Occupation	2,895,800	10,095,400	1,213,000	14,148,200
	Ratio (PUMS/Published)			
Population, 10 and Older	1.00	1.00	1.01	1.00
Recorded with Occupation	1.35	1.44	2.46	1.45
Recorded with no Occupation	0.97	0.91	0.93	0.92

Sources: The published figures were taken from the Department of the Interior, Census Office, *Statistics of the Population of the United States at the Tenth Census (June 1, 1880)*, Washington, D.C.: Government Printing Office, 1883, Table XXX:714. The enumerations were calculated from the 1880 manuscript census returns coded and documented by PUMS.

Table 2.2: Occupational Status of Females, 1900 Published Census Totals and the Public Use Microdata Sample (PUMS)

Age	10 to 15	16 to 64	65 and Older	Total
	Published Census			
Population, 10 and Older	4,767,374	21,926,128	1,526,321	28,219,823
Recorded with Occupation	486,137	4,686,253	138,691	5,311,081
Recorded with no Occupation	4,281,237	17,239,875	1,387,630	22,908,742
	Public Use Microdata Sample (PUMS*760)			
Population, 10 and Older	4,724,920	21,831,760	1,516,200	28,072,880
Recorded with Occupation	492,480	4,914,920	152,760	5,560,160
Recorded with no Occupation	4,232,440	16,916,840	1,363,440	22,512,720
	Ratio (PUMS/Published)			
Population, 10 and Older	0.99	1.00	0.99	0.99
Recorded with Occupation	1.01	1.05	1.10	1.05
Recorded with no Occupation	0.99	0.98	0.98	0.98

Sources: 1900 PUMS and 1900 Published Census.

Table 2.3: Occupational Status of Females, 1910 Published Census Totals and the Public use Microdata Sample (PUMS)

Age	10 to 15	16 to 44	45 and Older	Total
	Published Census			
Population, 10 and Older	5,364,137	20,964,270	8,224,305	34,552,712
Recorded with Occupation	637,086	6,150,569	1,288,117	8,075,772
Recorded with no Occupation	4,727,051	14,813,701	6,936,188	26,476,940
	Public Use Microdata Sample (PUMS*250)			
Population, 10 and Older	5,296,750	20,772,750	7,759,250	33,828,750
Recorded with Occupation	647,000	6,154,250	1,300,998	8,102,248
Recorded with no Occupation	4,649,750	14,618,500	6,458,252	25,726,502
	Ratio (PUMS/Published)			
Population, 10 and Older	0.99	0.99	0.94	0.98
Recorded with Occupation	1.02	1.00	1.01	1.00
Recorded with no Occupation	0.98	0.99	0.93	0.97

Sources: 1910 PUMS and 1910 Published Census.

Table 2.4: Percent of Married Women with Self-Employed Husbands (Farm and Non-Farm) or Boarders not Recorded as Gainful Workers in the Census, 1880-1910

Year	Women with Self-Employed Husbands	Additional Women in Households with Boarders
1880	57.2	3.3
1900	44.8	5.6
1910	25.6	6.7

Source: 1880 through 1910 PUMS.

Table 2.5: Upper-Bound Estimates of Married Women's Labor Force Participation Rates, 1880-1940 (percentages)

Year	Published Census	Additional Women in Self-Employed and Boarder Households	Revised Labor Force Participation Rate
1880	4.6	60.5	65.1
1900	5.6	50.4	56.0
1910	10.7	32.3	43.0
1940	26.9	n/a	26.9

Sources: Table 2.4 above and 1880 through 1910 Published Census.

Table 2.6: Comparison of the Labor Force Participation Rates for Married Women, PUMS, Published Census, and Upper-Bound Estimates, 1880-1910 (percentages)

Year	PUMS	Published Census[b]	Upper-Bound
1880/1890[a]	4.6	4.6	65.1
1900	5.3	5.6	56.0
1910	10.7	10.7	43.0

[a]There is no published estimate of the married female labor force participation rate for 1880, nor is there an 1890 estimate available in the PUMS. Therefore, the 1890 figure is used for the published census estimate and 1880 is used for the PUMS.

[b]Discrepancies between the PUMS estimates and those in the published census may be due to sampling error or, perhaps, editing by the Census Bureau (see Conk [1981], Carter and Sutch [1996], and Geib-Gundersen and Zahrt [1996]).

Sources: Table 2.5 above; 1880 through 1910 Published Census; and 1880 through 1910 PUMS.

NOTES

1. See footnote 1 in Chapter I for a discussion of the differences between the "gainful worker" concept prior to 1940 and the "labor force" concept used today.

2. Recall that the PUMS is not yet available for the years 1920 and 1930.

3. To be reviewed in the following section.

4. The adjustment methods discussed in this chapter are restricted to those aimed at analyzing married women's underenumeration. See Carter and Sutch (1996) for an analysis of biases inherent in the census returns for children and housewives.

5. Abel and Folbre (1990), p. 173.

6. Cited in Abel and Folbre (1990).

7. Bancroft (1958), Mincer (1966), Goldin (1990).

8. Women's Bureau of the Department of Labor.

9. These towns are Montague and Easthampton.

10. Abel and Folbre (1990), p. 171.

11. Abel and Folbre (1990), argue that Goldin's estimate is probably an underestimate since they believe that the 1910 census estimates cannot constitute an upper-bound. Furthermore, they claim that since men who worked less than part-time were included as labor force participants, women should not have been subject to the fifteen hour per week requirement. They note that virtually all men who lived on farms without off-farm employment were listed as farmers or farm laborers in the pre-1910 censuses.

12. See Conk (1981) for a detailed discussion of the types of changes that were made to enumerators' forms prior to the publication of census reports and, specifically, the removal of thousands of women from the gainful occupation classification. See Carter and Sutch (1996) and footnote 13, however, for doubts about Conk.

13. The PUMS is currently available for 1880, 1900, 1910, 1940, 1980, and 1990. It is commonly accepted in the literature that women's underenumeration is most problematic in the census years prior to the 1940 change in the definition of gainful work. Therefore, in this chapter I concentrate on the PUMS data available for 1880 through 1910.

14. Carter and Sutch (1996) discover that the Census Bureau edited the returns of the 1880 enumerators in a number of ways. One of interest for this book is the exclusion of women reporting their occupations as "Housekeeper" from the gainfully occupied category, despite instructions to enumerators that explicitly called for their inclusion. They find that by including Housekeepers in the gainful worker count, 12.3 percent of married women would be gainfully occupied according to the PUMS, rather than the 4.64 percent listed in the published census.

Chapter III

A History of Wives' Participation in Family Businesses

In Chapter II, upper-bound estimates of married women's labor force participation were generated in a manner that was consistent with the theory behind the traditional U-shape story. The driving force behind the high rates in the colonial period (the beginning of the U) is the inclusion of the wives of self-employed men. Therefore, one could argue that estimates of female labor force participation in later years must also include such women. Upper bound estimates were calculated through an examination of the recorded occupational status of women with self-employed husbands for the years of lowest portion of the U-shape. It was shown that the inclusion of *all* married women in self-employed households increases their labor force participation rate to 60.2 percent in 1880, 45.1 percent in 1900, 32.5 percent in 1910, and 21.1 percent in 1940.[1]

Is such an exhaustive inclusion appropriate? Perhaps not. While it may seem reasonable to assume that nearly 100 percent of farm wives performed farm labor for the market, such may not be the case for other occupations (say, contractors). The goal of this chapter is to provide a detailed examination of the particular occupations held by self-employed men in order to offer more accurate probabilities of their wives' involvement in family businesses. With these estimates, new adjustments are made to the labor force statistics on married women and implications drawn for the U-shaped pattern of participation over the course of the century.

The chapter begins with some descriptive statistics on self-employment from 1880 to 1940. Male participation rates in self-employment-intensive occupations are calculated for each year and the results categorized into four broad occupational groups: Farmers, Professionals, Entrepreneurs, and Retail Businessmen.[2] Next,I examine the recorded participation rates of the wives of men in each category and discover that an extremely large number of women with self-employed husbands were not recorded as having a gainful occupation.

The accuracy of this finding is addressed in two ways. First, I review the documentary evidence of the period on the nature of wives' participation in each of the different occupational categories identified above. Second, I estimate the number of excluded women that should be added to the labor force based on the more accurate recording procedure used in the 1940 data.[3] With this information, I make adjustments to married women's labor force participation rates that take into consideration the activities of wives in family businesses.

DESCRIPTIVE STATISTICS ON SELF-EMPLOYMENT

Table 3.1 shows, by race, the percentage of all married men engaged in self-employment in 1880, 1900, 1910, and 1940. This table illustrates both the dramatic racial differences in self-employment rates as well as the fact that by 1940, the rate of self-employment had declined—especially for white men.

An analysis of every single occupation in which men found self-employment around the turn of the century would be extremely tedious and offer little insight. Therefore, I facilitate my examination of particular occupations by employing the categorization of self-employment-intensive occupations suggested by Carter and Sutch (1996, Appendix A) since over 90 percent of all self-employed men were located here in 1910. The occupations are listed in Table 3.2 for 1880 through 1910, in Table 3.3 for 1940, and are grouped into the categories mentioned in the first section: Farmers, Professionals, Entrepreneurs, and Retail Businessmen. These tables list the number of self-employed, married males in the most self-employment-intensive occupations, by category,in each year.As can be seen,the overwhelming majority of men in self-employment-intensive occupations were in the agricultural sector. The extreme racial disparities in rates of self-employment are highlighted in Tables 3.4 through 3.7 in which the figures from Tables 3.2 and 3.3 are disaggregated by race for each year (the implications of this racial division are the subject of Chapter IV).

Tables 3.8 and 3.9 identify, again by race and occupational category, the recorded participation rates of women with self-employed husbands. As can be seen, in 1880, 21.0 percent of black farm wives were recorded as gainfully occupied, while a mere 0.5 percent of white farm wives were recorded as such. In 1900, the figures are 19.4 percent for black farm wives and 1.3 percent for white farm wives and in 1910, they are 32.1 percent for black farm wives and 3.6 percent for white farm wives. The recorded participation rates of women in the other three occupational categories are listed in the tables.

In 1940, due to the change in census enumeration procedures that made women's work in family businesses more visible (and thus, more often counted), the percentages are significantly higher: 64.3 percent of black farm wives and 36.1 percent of white wives were recorded as employed. Note, however, that by 1940, whether a woman's husband was self-employed had an insignificant effect on her recorded labor force status (see Table 3.10), implying in part that such wives were less frequently overlooked than in the earlier years, when unpaid family workers were the most undercounted group.[4] Therefore, the revisions to married women's labor force participation rates in this chapter will exploit the accuracy of the 1940 data to reestimate the more problematic rates from 1880 to 1910. My objective is to determine whether the exclusion of self-employed wives from the early census employment statistics was consistent with the instructions given to enumerators.

Why would one suspect that such an exclusion might not be appropriate? Robert Smuts raises suspicion of the census statistics in the following comment:

"... there is still some question about the accuracy of the Census count of women workers [in the data for 1930 and earlier years]. Some members of the labor force inevitably escape enumeration. It is generally acknowledged that this is most likely to happen when counting women and children who work irregularly, especially if they are unpaid workers on a family farm or in a family business."[5]

Recall that in Chapter I, a chart was presented (Figure 1.2) that demonstrated how the sex division of labor of the period and the instructions to enumerators could combine to classify automatically all men in small enterprises as self-employed proprietors and their wives as either unpaid family assistants or, more commonly, as housewives. This might be the case even if the actual work performed by the husband and wife was indistinguishable and the time spent equivalent. Such automatic assignment by enumerators would both obscure the actual division of labor in the family business and misrepresent women's economic contributions to society as a whole. That the PUMS shows *no* married men as unpaid family workers and very few wives as self-employed suggests that the sex division of labor for this category of employment may have been structured according to ideology of the era, rather than the reality of people's work situations.[6]

In the section that follows, I present a collection of documentary evidence from the turn of the century that gives a first-hand indication of the activities in which wives in family businesses were engaged. In order to help determine the probability that wives participated in the operation of their family's particular type of business, I examine this evidence in each of the four occupational categories described above.

DOCUMENTARY EVIDENCE

An enormous body of literature on the history of self-employment suggests that the wives of self-employed men were not merely idle observers of their husbands' business activities.[7] Rather, most or all of the workers in a family business were members of the owner's family who performed bookkeeping activities, staffed stores, and produced output. This literature makes it clear that women were, in general, active participants in the operation of their families' businesses.

Although a wife's work was oriented toward the market and clearly of the GNP-producing type considered "gainful" by census definitions of employment, it was done privately within the family for her husband. The woman worked as a wife, not a wage-earner or petty producer. The husband supervised the family business and was its public representative.[8] Hence, it is not surprising that these women were usually overlooked by census enumerators. Because the extent of this underenumeration most likely varied across the occupational categories defined above, I turn now to an examination of the literature for each such group. I begin with the literature on farmers' wives and then turn to the wives of Professionals, Entrepreneurs, and Retail Businessmen.

THE WIVES OF FARMERS:

The *Farmer's Wife* was a journal published from 1905 until 1946 aimed at providing advice and information for women who lived on farms. This journal is a rich source of details on the lives and daily activities of these women. In the July 1928 issue, for example, the *Farmer's Wife* published an article entitled, "A Portrait: The Typical Farm Homemaker," that depicted farm wives as truly equal partners in the farm business by claiming that "The woman on the farm is in the very center of the farm business and knows the details of sowing and planing, of harvesting and marketing the crops just as intimately as her husband."

Women had a variety of responsibilities on their farms. Tending to poultry, we learn from the *Farmer's Wife*, was a major one. Letters to the journal attest to this, such as the one from "Out of Breath Betty," who asked,

> Is it really worth while to try to do the work of two or three women in a day? It is two or three, isn't it, when a woman does all the necessary work in a home and then helps her husband in the field, and raises a hundred chickens?"[9]

and a similar one from a Kansas woman,

> This is my question: When I have cooked, and swept, and washed, and ironed, and made beds for a family of five . . . and have done the necessary mending and some sewing, haven't I done enough? In any fair division of labor between the farmer and his wife the man would take the outdoors and the woman the indoors. That would drop the chickens on the man's side, with the probable result that on most farms there would be no chickens."[10]

These writings are supported by a 1910 farm census which revealed that 88 percent of farms raised chickens, with an average of 80.4 chickens per farm, and that 70 percent of poultry production was carried out by women.[11] Other responsibilities of farm wives are illustrated in the results of a 1919 USDA survey on their activities. The survey found that farm women participated in the following activities at the rates indicated below:[12]

Activity	Wives Engaged
Helps to milk cows	36%
Makes butter	60%
Sells butter	33%
Cares for poultry	81%
Average size of flock	90 hens
Carries water	61%
Distance water carried	65 ft.
Helps in fields	24%
Cares for garden	56%

It is clear from this evidence that the wives of farmers did, in fact, participate in the activities of their family's business, most likely to a greater extent that was recorded in the censuses of 1880 through 1910 (a mere 0.5 percent, 1.3 percent, and 3.6 percent of white wives in each census year), but perhaps to a lesser extent than is suggested by Ciancanelli (1983).[13] New estimates of this participation are presented in the next section, in light of the documentary evidence reviewed here.

THE WIVES OF PROFESSIONALS:

Extremely little has been written about the economic activities of the wives of men in occupations such as dentists, lawyers and judges, and physicians. Virginia Penny (1863) writes in *The Employments of Women: A Cyclopadia of Woman's Work* that "many wives of professional men learn bookkeeping, that they may keep their husbands' books." Without providing much more information on *how* many wives this employment may have involved, Peterson (1929) gives a similar account when he states that ". . . a number of these men [professionals and entrepreneurs] had the intelligence to use as book keepers their own wives, thus saving themselves the expense of a hired office girl."

It is difficult to determine the magnitude these authors meant to suggest when they wrote "many wives" and "a number of these men." However, it is likely that they meant something a bit more substantial than the 0.9 to 1.8 percent rates that were recorded in the censuses of 1880 through 1910 for professionals' wives.

No evidence was found that wives assisted their husbands as medical or dental assistants or secretaries, rather, these services were normally provided by other, unmarried women trained in such capacities.

THE WIVES OF ENTREPRENEURS:

The situation for the wives of self-employed builders, contractors, and manufacturers is very similar to that for professionals' in that there is a dearth of documentary evidence about their activities. However, to roughly the same extent as professionals, it seems that these wives frequently acted as accountants or bookkeepers for their husbands' businesses (recall that Peterson wrote of both professionals' and entrepreneurs' wives). Consider the writings of Mrs. Montague, whose husband was a northern coal mine owner, which indicate a substantial amount of time spent in bookkeeping activities for her husband's business:

> "Business has taken up much of my time . . . So now, as soon as I can get the ends and bottoms of our business wound up, I shall set out for Hill St. I have almost put my eyes out with accounts, of which our steward brings a plentiful quantity at this time of year. He [expects] that I will apply many hours in the day. Our affairs go on very prosperously and in great order, so that I have as little trouble as is possible in a case where so many large accounts are to be look'd over."[14]

The recorded rates for the wives of entrepreneurs in the census occupation statistics are 1.9 percent, 0.5 percent, and 2.3 percent in 1880 through 1910. The accuracy of these rates is examined in the following section.

THE WIVES OF RETAIL BUSINESSMEN:

The evidence on wives' activities in their families' retail, hotel, and restaurant establishments is more prevalent. We learn clearly that when men's wage work took place in the household itself, wives were often expected to integrate into their own schedules substantial aspects of their husbands' occupations. The wife of a man who turned one of their rooms into a storefront or their home into an inn generally anticipated, as Benjamin Franklin noted, that his wife would "assist by tending shop."[15]

Many middle-class and working-class women appear to have spent considerable time working in shops that their husbands presumably owned and operated, saving the business the costs that would otherwise have been paid in wages to a clerk. William Bell, a police officer in New York City in the 1900s whose duties included citing small businesses for operating without a license, discovered that many of the shops he visited were often staffed by women. When he "Called at Wm. P. Bennett('s) Second Hand Clothing Store" for example, Bell found Bennett's wife running the shop—and apparently functioning as its full proprietor, since she claimed that she had stocked the store, buying "her goods exclusively at Auction."[16]

Many references to such instances can also be found in the writings of women themselves. Anne Bryant Smith of Portsmouth, Maine, waited on customers and helped purchase the stock for her husband's shop. She was, according to her diary, both "Maid about house, and Cleark in the store."[17] "Attending the store" was a common occurrence for Sarah Campbell, whose other responsibilities included caring for her six children. Similarly, in her husband's absence, Anna Jackson Lowell, who had children, housework, and a school to attend to, wrote that she also often minded the family store.[18]

That many women were fully knowledgeable about the functionings of their family's business is indicated by the numerous legal advertisements announcing that a widow would be taking over ownership and operation of her deceased husband's firm. In fact, wives were usually so well acquainted with their husband's business as to be "mistress of the managing part of it" and able to carry on in his absence or after his death.[19] Below is part of a letter, sent by the widows of New York to their local newspaper in 1893, demanding their rights as property-owners and citizens. It suggests that many of the New York widows supported themselves through shopkeeping:

> Mr. Zenger,
>
>   We, the widdows of this city, have had a Meeting, and as our case is something Deplorable, we beg you will give it Place in your Weekly Journal, that we may be Relieved, it is as follows.
>
>   We are House keepers, Pay our Taxes, carry on Trade, and most of us are she Merchants . . .[20]

It is difficult to determine, from the documentary evidence on the wives of retail businessmen, exactly what percentage of women actually performed work in their family's stores. However, census figures of 4.1 percent, 3.8 percent, and 14.2 percent from 1880 to 1910 are, most likely, significant underestimates.

UNCOVERING THE HIDDEN WORK OF WOMEN IN FAMILY BUSINESSES

The documentary evidence of the previous section is now combined with an empirical analysis of the PUMS census data. The theoretical framework and objective of this chapter can perhaps best be understood through the use of a diagram (Figure 3.1). This figure illustrates that within the group of all married women, we can identify the subset classified as gainfully occupied by census enumerators, the subset married to self-employed men, and the intersection of these two subsets—those women with self-employed husbands who were themselves also classified as gainfully occupied.

It is necessary, however, to further subdivide the group of women contained in this intersection—the gainfully occupied women with self-employed husbands. It is possible that a woman's husband was self-employed and that she was counted as gainfully occupied, but in an occupation not related to her family's business (say, a contractor's wife who was a seamstress). These are not the women of interest in this chapter since my goal is to gain more insight into women's activities *within* family businesses. Figure 3.1 highlights the two groups to be considered in this section, labeled **A** and **B**. Group **A** includes those women with self-employed husbands who were recorded as having a gainful occupation that was related to her family's business.[21] Group **B** includes those women with self-employed husbands who were not recorded as having a gainful occupation themselves.

Because a woman's recorded occupational status was most likely affected by enumerator bias (which was in turn affected by the ideology of the era), it is probably the case that a number of women were not placed in the appropriate group by census enumerators. Clearly, within Group **B** there are some women who are legitimately not in the labor force. However, it may be the case that there are some women in this group who, by participating in their family's businesses, should have been classified as gainfully occupied and placed in Group **A**. These are the women I seek to identify by employing a procedure that utilizes information from the PUMS and the census of 1940.

REVISING THE PARTICIPATION RATES OF MARRIED WOMEN

Recall from Chapter II that the census of 1940 marked the beginning of greater accuracy in employment statistics. Before 1940, a respondent was counted as gainfully occupied if he or she reported having an occupation. Beginning in 1940, the current definition of labor force participation was adopted and respondents were counted as gainfully occupied if they reported having worked for wages for at least one hour during the previous week, working as an unpaid family worker for at least fifteen hours, or actively looking for employment during the previous week. Therefore, since activities—rather than occupations— were the subject of inquiry in 1940, the data on married women's labor force participation in this year is commonly viewed as more accurate than the pre-1940 data.

Referring back to Tables 3.8 and 3.9, we see that the rate at which wives of self-employed men were recorded as employed in occupations related to their husband's business was much higher in 1940 than in the earlier years. However, there are several reasons to believe that such participation by wives from 1880 to 1910 was *at least as high* as it was in 1940.

First, self-employed Farmers and Retail Businessmen each formed a larger proportion of all self-employed men earlier in the century. As a group, they were both more numerous and more likely to use wives in their businesses than those in 1940.[22]

Second, on average, small businesses were more labor intensive before 1940 so it is possible that a larger number of these entrepreneurs required a greater amount of family labor.[23]

Finally, residential patterns in 1940 were quite different from those around the turn of the century. In the earlier years, there were much shorter distances between home and work. Fewer families lived upstairs their stores and businesses. Since location is hypothesized as a major variable in the work patterns of wives, their greater proximity to the family enterprise from 1880 to 1910 may have induced or facilitated a larger proportion of them to work as unpaid family assistants.[24]

These changes in the occupational distribution of the self-employed from 1880 to 1940, which impacted the use of wives' labor, imply that using the 1940 participation rates for each occupational category as proxies for the true participation rates from 1880 to 1910 will likely *understate* the true contributions of married women in family businesses. With this possible underestimation in mind, I turn now to an examination of the reliability of the 1940 data on married women's occupational status. Table 3.11 shows that by using probit estimation and the PUMS data, we are able to make extremely reliable predictions of the recorded employment status of married women in 1940. This table lists the sample mean and probit coefficients for a probit regression determining whether a woman was recorded as having an occupation related to her husband's business, given that her husband was self-employed. This prediction procedure is described below.

The documentary evidence reviewed above indicates that participation by wives in their family's business was sensitive to the particular occupation of their husband. We found, for example, that wives of farmers and retail businessmen appeared to have been much more likely to participate than wives of professionals and entrepreneurs. The evidence also suggests that this participation was also influenced by whether a woman's husband was an *employer* (hired workers in his business) or *worked on his own account* (with no paid employees).[25] It seems as though a man would be most likely to employ his wife as an unpaid family worker if he was working on his own account, rather than as an employer. Therefore, the independent variables used in this procedure include dummies representing the husband's occupational status, his class of worker status (employer or own account), as well as three interactive terms capturing the effect of the husband's class of worker status by occupational category. In addition to these variables, I include the following: the woman's race and age, whether her husband experienced a spell of unemployment, whether she lived in the South, whether she lived in an urban or rural area, her health status, the presence of children under the age of five, her nativity, the presence of boarders and servants, and whether her family owned their home.

As can be seen, the probit equation has a great deal of explanatory power: nearly 94 percent of the observations are predicted correctly as determined using within-sample prediction tests. Furthermore, most of the variables are significant and have the expected signs. We find, for example, that a woman is most likely to have been recorded as employed in an occupation related to her family's business if she was a white, her husband was either a farmer or retail businessman, she lived in the South, did not have young children, and her husband worked on his own account, rather than being an employer. The interactive terms indicate that the husband's class of worker status was more important for farmers and entrepreneurs than retail businessmen or professionals in determining whether a woman participated in the operation of her family's business.

The results of this estimation procedure are presented in Table 3.12. This table shows that in 1940, the rate at which black farm wives were recorded as participating in their husbands' business was 44.3 percent, and for white farm wives it was 46.1 percent. For the wives of professionals, we find participation rates in their husbands' business of 2.7 percent for black women and 13.9 percent for white women. The rates for entrepreneurs are 1.4 percent for black wives and 12.0 percent for white wives. Finally, retail businessmen's wives participated in their operations at rates of 20.8 percent for black women and 48.3 percent for white women. *Note that these rates correspond very closely to those suggested by the documentary evidence discussed above for wives from 1880 to 1910.*

Assuming that the actual (as opposed to the recorded) rate of participation for such wives in each occupational category from 1880 to 1910 was at least as high as those in 1940, we find that fully 33.5 percent of all white, married women would be added to the labor force in 1880, 30.4 percent in 1900, and 26.1 percent in 1910. The corresponding figures for black wives are 10.2 percent, 9.7 percent, and 8.6 percent. The lower percentages for black women reflect both the fact that they were less likely to live with self-employed men and that they were enumerated more accurately at the time the census was taken. Adding these estimates to the recorded labor force participation rate for white wives gives the strikingly revised participation rates of 35.2 percent in 1880, 32.7 percent in 1900, and 32.4 percent in 1910. The revised rates for black wives are 38.4 percent in 1880, 31.8 percent in 1900, and 39.9 percent in 1910. These rates are given by occupational category in the tables.

Accounting for differences in the propensity to work in a family business radically changes the pattern of married women's labor force participation over the course of the century, as is illustrated in Figures

3.2 and 3.3. Also of note is the fact that the revised rates close the racial participation gap significantly; the implications of this fact are the subject of Chapter IV.

IMPLICATIONS FOR THE U-SHAPED PATTERN OF MARRIED WOMEN'S LABOR FORCE PARTICIPATION

With the revised estimates of married women's labor force status, a new pattern of participation emerges that is different from the traditional U-shape story around the turn of the century. Figure 3.3 indicates that, as opposed to initially falling then rising participation rates, the more accurate pattern may be one of relative constancy across the century, marked by high participation rates in 1880, 1900, and 1910 (the traditional bottom of the "U"), a subsequent decline in 1940 as self-employment became less common, and a gradual increase in participation after 1940 as more educated women began to enter the paid labor force.

It is important to keep in mind, however, that the results obtained in this chapter are *underestimates* of married women's true participation rate. Therefore, the revised pattern of participation, as indicated in Figure 3.3, is biased toward implying that the rate at which married women's were involved in the labor force did not change over the course of the century. In fact, we know that the true pattern of married women's participation was marked by higher rates around the turn of the century than those indicated in this chapter due to the fact that we have not captured *all* of the occupations in which men were self-employed. Given that the rates of participation between 1880 and 1910 were *at least as high* as those in 1940 (which are taken to be accurate as recorded by census enumerators), and that the rates in 1940 were *lower* than those after 1940, we can surmise that the actual "bottom of the U", or the point at which married women's labor force participation was the lowest, occurred in 1940.[26] Once the PUMS becomes available for the years 1920 and 1930, this finding can be verified and analyzed in more detail, but for now this is left as an avenue for further research.

APPENDIX A: THE IDENTIFICATION OF SELF-EMPLOYMENT-INTENSIVE OCCUPATIONS

The method of identifying self-employment-intensive occupations in this chapter follows that of Carter and Sutch (1996, Appendix A) and is recounted briefly here.[27] The 1910 census was the first to ask individuals to classify their employment status as either "Employer", "Works on Own Account", or "Employee". However, these results were never tabulated or published, and have only become available with the release of the Public Use Microdata Sample of manuscript returns.

The Census Bureau defined an "Employer" as one who "employs helpers, other than domestic servants, in transacting his own business".[28] "Employee" included "any person who works for wages or a salary and is subject to the control and direction of an employer".[29] Finally, an individual recording his or her status as "Works on Own Account" was to include anyone with a gainful occupation who were neither employers nor employees.[30] Carter and Sutch point out that the Census Instructions to Enumerators mentioned several examples:

> Farmers and the owners of small establishments who do not employ helpers; professional men who work for fees and employ no helpers; and, generally speaking, hucksters, peddlers, newsboys, bootblacks, etc., although it not infrequently happens that persons in these pursuits are employed by others and are working for wages, and in such case should, of course, be returned as employees.

Using this "employment status" variable in the 1910 PUMS, Carter and Sutch identify those occupations that are the most self-employment-intensive; i.e., those that contain the highest percentage of self-employed respondents. I extend this categorization to 1880 and 1900 by assuming that the same occupations were self-employment-intensive in these years as in 1910 (since employment status variables are not available). By construction, then, 100 percent of the workers in self-employment-intensive occupations in 1880 and 1900 are self-employed.

Figure 3.1: Married Women's Spheres

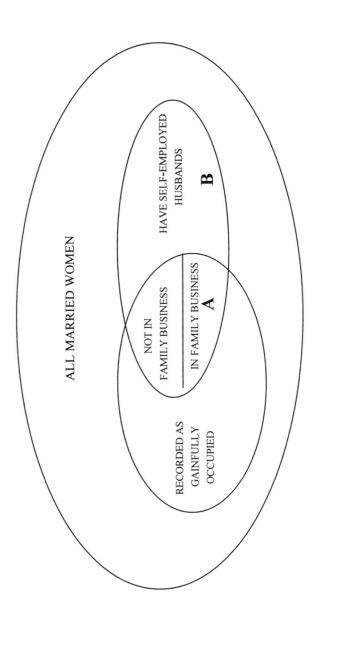

Figure 3.2: Standard Estimates of the U-Shaped Pattern of Married Women's Labor Force Participation Rates

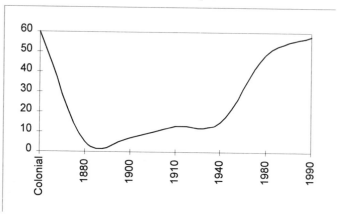

Figure 3.3: Revised Estimates of Married Women's Labor Force Participation Rates

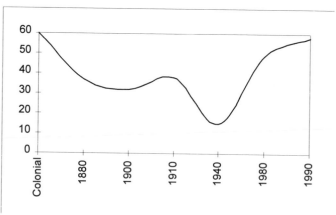

Table 3.1: Self-Employment Rates of Married Males in the U.S., by Race, 1880-1940

	1880	1900	1910	1940
Black	21.6	21.3	19.1	16.9
White	52.8	46.7	39.0	18.4

Notes: Questions about self-employment were not asked in the 1880 and 1900 censuses and had to be imputed using a method which predicts self-employment by identifying the most self-employment intensive occupations in 1910 (see Appendix A in this chapter and Carter and Sutch [1996a]). This technique underestimates the self-employment rate in 1880 and 1900 since it excludes workers in occupations that were not self-employment-intensive, such as carpenters and tailors.

Table 3.2: Number of Self-Employed, Married Males by Occupation and Occupation Group (Self-Employment-Intensive Occupations) 1880, 1900 and 1910

Occupation	Number			% Self-Empl.
	1880	1900	1910	in 1910
Farmers:				
Dairy farmers	5,200	*a*	48,000	100.0
Farmers	3,538,400	4,314,520	4,728,500	99.9
Florists	2,400	10,640	7,250	100.0
Fruit growers	*a*	8,360	37,750	100.0
Gardeners	29,100	34,200	66,000	100.0
Stock Raisers	10,200	28,120	46,000	100.0
Total	*3,585,300*	*4,395,840*	*4,933,500*	*99.9*
Professionals:				
Dentists	7,500	15,200	28,500	87.7
Lawyers and judges	42,100	67,640	78,000	87.2
Physicians and surgeons	62,400	83,600	103,500	91.1
Veterinary surgeons	2,000	9,120	7,250	89.7
Total	*114,000*	*175,560*	*217,250*	*89.2*
Entrepreneurs:				
Builders and contractors	10,400	37,240	117,000	95.7
Manufacturers	40,400	116,280	194,000	97.6
Total	*50,800*	*153,520*	*311,000*	*96.9*
Retail Businessmen:				
Livery stable keepers	11,800	13,680	27,750	91.9
Real estate agents	9,600	76,000	93,000	83.6
Retail dealers	351,500	457,520	858,000	87.9
Wholesale dealers	*b*	46,360	42,750	87.7
Hotel keepers	21,600	40,280	45,250	82.9
Restaurant keepers	8,600	9,120	39,000	87.8
Saloon keepers	44,200	50,920	47,500	95.8
Total	*447,300*	*693,880*	*1,153,250*	*87.8*
Total:	*4,197,400*	*5,418,800*	*6,615,000*	*97.3*

[a] Included with farmers.

[b] No distinction is made between retail and wholesale dealers in 1880.

Table 3.3: Number of Self-Employed, Married Males by Occupation and Occupation Group (Self-Employment-Intensive Occupations) 1940

Occupation	Number	% Self-Employed
Farmers:		
Farmers	4,078,425	99.6
Livestock buyers and shippers	15,600	84.2
Gardeners	14,625	60.0
Total	*4,108,650*	*97.0*
Professionals:		
Dentists	50,700	94.5
Lawyers and judges	85,800	74.6
Physicians and surgeons	109,200	86.2
Chiropractors	8,775	100.0
Healers and medical service workers (n.e.c.)	6,825	70.0
Optometrists	5,850	100.0
Total	*267,150*	*83.5*
Entrepreneurs:		
Builders	2,925	75.0
Contractors	109,200	65.9
Manufacturers	3,900	80.0
Total	*116,025*	*66.1*
Retail Businessmen:		
Hucksters and peddlers	25,350	81.1
Auctioneers	2,925	75.0
Shoemakers and repairers	52,650	83.1
Total	*80,925*	*83.0*
Total:	*4,572,750*	*94.7*

Table 3.4: Number of Self-Employed, Married Males by Race, Occupation and Occupation Group, 1880

Occupation	Number		% of All Workers	
	Black	White	Black	White
Farmers:				
Dairy farmers	0	5,200	0.0	0.1
Farmers	158,300	3,167,300	19.2	43.2
Florists	0	2,400	0.0	0.03
Fruit growers	*a*	—	—	—
Gardeners	2,500	26,100	0.3	0.4
Stock Raisers	200	9,700	0.0	0.1
Total	*161,000*	*3,210,700*	*19.5*	*43.8*
Professionals:				
Dentists	0	7,500	0.0	0.1
Lawyers and judges	200	41,900	0.02	0.6
Physicians and surgeons	100	62,100	0.01	0.8
Veterinary surgeons	0	1,900	0.0	0.03
Total	*300*	*113,400*	*0.03*	*1.5*
Entrepreneurs:				
Builders and contractors	200	10,200	0.02	0.1
Manufacturers	100	40,200	0.01	0.5
Total	*300*	*50,400*	*0.03*	*0.6*
Retail Businessmen:				
Livery stable keepers	200	11,500	0.02	0.2
Real estate agents	0	9,600	0.0	0.1
Retail dealers	1,500	348,600	0.2	4.8
Wholesale dealers	*b*	—	—	—
Hotel keepers	0	21,500	0.0	0.3
Restaurant keepers	500	8,100	0.06	0.1
Saloon keepers	1,100	42,600	0.1	0.6
Total	*3,300*	*441,900*	*0.4*	*6.1*
All Other Occupations:			*1.6*	*0.8*
Total:	*164,900*	*3,816,400*	*23.6*	*52.8*

a Included with farmers.

b No distinction is made between retail and wholesale dealers in 1880.

Table 3.5: Number of Self-Employed, Married Males by Race, Occupation and Occupation Group, 1900

Occupation	Number Black	Number White	% of All Workers Black	% of All Workers White
Farmers:				
Dairy farmers	a	—	—	—
Farmers	228,000	3,743,000	18.6	33.7
Florists	760	9,880	0.06	0.09
Fruit growers	0	7,600	0.0	0.07
Gardeners	1,520	32,680	0.1	0.3
Stock Raisers	0	28,120	0.0	0.3
Total	*230,280*	*3,821,280*	*18.8*	*34.5*
Professionals:				
Dentists	0	15,200	0.0	0.1
Lawyers and judges	760	66,120	0.06	0.6
Physicians and surgeons	0	83,600	0.0	0.8
Veterinary surgeons	0	9,120	0.0	0.08
Total	*760*	*174,040*	*0.06*	*1.6*
Entrepreneurs:				
Builders and contractors	760	34,960	0.06	0.4
Manufacturers	0	116,280	0.0	1.0
Total	*760*	*151,240*	*0.06*	*1.4*
Retail Businessmen:				
Livery stable keepers	1,520	12,160	0.1	0.1
Real estate agents	0	76,000	0.0	0.7
Retail dealers	6,840	450,680	0.6	4.1
Wholesale dealers	760	45,600	0.06	0.4
Hotel keepers	0	40,280	0.0	0.4
Restaurant keepers	0	9,120	0.0	0.08
Saloon keepers	1,520	49,400	0.1	0.5
Total	*10,640*	*683,240*	*0.9*	*6.3*
All Other Occupations:			*1.5*	*2.9*
Total:	*242,440*	*4,829,800*	*21.3*	*46.7*

a Included with farmers.

Table 3.6: Number of Self-Employed, Married Males by Race, Occupation and Occupation Group, 1910

Occupation	Number		% of All Workers	
	Black	White	Black	White
Farmers:				
Dairy farmers	0	48,000	0.0	0.2
Farmers	425,500	3,991,000	16.5	27.6
Florists	250	7,000	0.01	0.03
Fruit growers	250	37,000	0.01	1.4
Gardeners	1,500	62,250	0.1	2.3
Stock Raisers	500	42,750	0.02	0.2
Total	*428,000*	*4,188,000*	*16.6*	*31.7*
Professionals:				
Dentists	500	27,500	0.02	0.1
Lawyers and judges	0	77,250	0.0	0.3
Physicians and surgeons	500	102,250	0.02	0.4
Veterinary surgeons	0	7,250	0.0	0.03
Total	*1,000*	*214,250*	*0.04*	*0.8*
Entrepreneurs:				
Builders and contractors	1,000	115,250	0.04	0.4
Manufacturers	500	192,250	0.02	0.7
Total	*1,500*	*307,500*	*0.06*	*1.1*
Retail Businessmen:				
Livery stable keepers	250	27,500	0.02	0.1
Real estate agents	250	92,500	0.02	0.3
Retail dealers	7,250	839,750	0.3	3.2
Wholesale dealers	250	42,500	0.01	0.2
Hotel keepers	750	43,500	0.03	0.2
Restaurant keepers	1,500	35,000	0.1	0.1
Saloon keepers	0	47,500	0.0	0.2
Total	*10,250*	*1,128,250*	*0.5*	*4.3*
All Other Occupations:			*1.9*	*1.1*
Total:	*440,750*	*5,838,000*	*19.1*	*39.0*

Table 3.7: Number of Self-Employed, Married Males by Race, Occupation and Occupation Group (Self-Employment-Intensive Occupations), 1940

Occupation	Number Black	White	% of All Workers Black	White
Farmers:				
Farmers	298,350	3,537,300	14.0	15.1
Livestock buyers	0	18,525	0	0.1
Gardeners	17,550	104,325	0.8	0.4
Total	*315,900*	*3,660,150*	*14.8*	*15.6*
Professionals:				
Dentists	4,875	48,750	0.2	0.2
Lawyers and judges	975	114,075	0.05	0.5
Physicians and surgeons	4,875	121,875	0.2	0.5
Chiropractors	0	8,775	0	0.03
Healers and medical service workers (n.e.c.)	1,950	7,800	0.1	0.03
Optometrists	0	5,850	0	0.02
Total	*12,675*	*307,125*	*0.6*	*1.3*
Entrepreneurs:				
Builders	975	2,925	0.05	0.01
Contractors	13,650	153,075	0.6	0.7
Manufacturers	0	4,875	0	0.02
Total	*14,625*	*160,875*	*0.7*	*0.7*
Retail Businessmen:				
Hucksters and peddlers	2,925	27,300	0.1	0.1
Auctioneers	0	3,900	0	0.01
Shoemakers and repairers	4,875	58,500	0.2	0.2
Total	*7,800*	*89,700*	*0.3*	*0.3*
All Other Occupations:			0.5	0.5
Total:	*589,875*	*4,217,850*	*16.9*	*18.4*

Table 3.8: Labor Force Participation Rate of Women with Self-Employed Husbands, by Race and Self-Employment-Intensive Occupation Group, 1880 and 1900

| | Labor Force Participation Rate | | | |
| | 1880 | | 1900 | |
	Black	White	Black	White
All Married Women:	28.2	1.7	22.1	2.3
Women with Husbands who are				
Farmers:	21.0	0.5	19.4	1.3
Professionals:	*	1.8	*	0.9
Entrepreneurs:	*	1.9	*	0.5
Retail Businessmen:	29.0	4.1	15.4	3.8

* Small sample size.

Table 3.9: Labor Force Participation Rate of Women with Self-Employed Husbands, by Race and Self-Employment-Intensive Occupation Group, 1910 and 1940

| | Labor Force Participation Rate | | | |
| | 1910 | | 1940 | |
	Black	White	Black	White
All Married Women:	41.3	6.3	24.6	12.4
Women with Husbands who are				
Farmers:	32.1	3.6	44.3	36.1
Professionals:	*	1.8	2.7	13.9
Entrepreneurs:	*	2.3	1.4	12.0
Retail Businessmen:	22.6	14.2	20.8	36.3

* Small sample size.

Table 3.10: Probit Coefficients (Dichotomous Dependent Variable: Employment Status of Wives), Sample: All Married Women, 1940

Independent Variable	Coefficient
Race *(black=1, white=0)*	2.81*
Husband is self-employed	-.17
Age:[a]	
15-24	.48
25-29	.21*
30-34	.59*
35-39	.44*
40-49	.19*
In poor health	-1.02*
Has children less than 5 years old	-.22*
Foreign born	.45*
Has boarders in household	-.26*
Has servants in household	-.18
Lives in urban area	.81*
Lives in the South	.56*

* Significant at the 95 percent level.

[a] Age 50 and over is the reference category.

**Table 3.11: Probit Coefficients and Summary Statistics
(Dichotomous Dependent Variable = 1 if Wife is Employed in
Occupation Related to Husband's Business, Zero Otherwise)
Sample: Wives of Self-Employed Men, 1940**

Independent Variable	Sample Mean	Coefficient
Constant	—	-1.29
Race (*black = 1, white = 0*)	.07	-.87*
Age 15-24	.09	-.43*
25-29	.16	.62*
30-34	.31	.71*
35-39	.20	.73*
40-49[a]	.14	.38*
Husband self-employed as:		
Farmer	.90	2.01*
Entrepreneur	.03	.14*
Retail Businessman[b]	.02	2.89*
Months husband unemployed	1.2	.95*
Lives in South	.54	.72*
Lives in urban area	.23	.10*
In poor health	.04	-.36
Has children less than 5 years old	.48	-.22*
Foreign born	.04	.44*
Has boarders in household	.03	-.37*
Has servants in household	.01	-.29
Owns home	.37	.07
Husband's class of worker status		
(*employer = 1, own account = 0*)	.36	-.91*
Class of worker * Farmer	—	-.35*
Class of worker * Entrepreneur	—	-.09*
Class of worker * Retail Businessman[c]	—	-.26*
-2 x LLR[d]	—	161.9
Percentage predicted correctly	—	93.8

Notes to Table 3.11:

* Significant at the 95 percent level.

[a] Age 50 and over is the omitted category.

[b] Professional is the omitted category.

[c] Class of worker * professional is the omitted category.

[d] Minus two times the log likelihood ratio, which has the chi-squared distribution with 24 degrees of freedom. The null hypothesis is that all coefficients are zero.

Table 3.12: Revised Labor Force Participation Rates of Married Women, by Race and Self-Employment-Intensive Occupation Group, 1880-1910

	1880		1900		1910	
	Blk	Wht	Blk	Wht	Blk	Wht
Recorded Participation Rate						
(% of all married women):	28.2	1.7	22.1	2.3	31.3	6.3
	Average for 1880 through 1910 (based on 1940 rates)					
Women with Husbands who are		*Black*			*White*	
Farmers:		44.3			46.1	
Professionals:		2.7			13.9	
Entrepreneurs:		1.4			12.0	
Retail Businessmen:		20.8			48.3	
Total to Add						
(% of all married women): [a]	10.2	33.5	9.7	30.4	8.6	26.1
Revised Participation Rate	*38.4*	*35.2*	*31.8*	*32.7*	*39.9*	*32.4*
(% of all married women):						

[a] Calculated using the PUMS (1880 through 1940) and estimates in Tables 3.8 and 3.9.

NOTES

1. These revised figures, while called "upper-bound" estimates due to the fact that *all* married women in self-employed households are added to the labor force, are in fact underestimates of married women's participation rate for two reasons. First, the technique used to predict a husband's self-employment status using the recorded rates in 1910 underestimates the extent of self-employment in 1880 and 1900 due to the fact that certain occupations were self-employment-intensive in these earlier years that were not in 1910 (see Appendix A). Second, this method leaves out other forms of often uncounted market work in which married women participated such as keeping boarders, taking in factory piece work, and laundering. Recall that the PUMS is not available for 1920 and 1930. Furthermore, two factors suggest that the exclusion of women with self-employed husbands was significantly less

problematic in 1940 and later years. The first is the change in the definition of gainful work implemented in 1940 that made census statistics on employment more inclusive of women's work (see Chapter I for a discussion). Second, the declining rate of self-employment by 1940 meant that significantly fewer women even had self-employed husbands (see Table 3.1 in this chapter).

2. These are the occupational categories suggested by Carter and Sutch (1996).

3. The ways in which the 1940 data are more accurate are discussed below.

4. This finding is discussed in detail in Chapter II.

5. Smuts (1959), p. 159.

6. Ciancanelli (1983), p. 48 and PUMS (1880 through 1940).

7. Specific references are cited throughout this section.

8. Matthaei (1982).

9. *Farmer's Wife* (1919), 18.

10. *Farmer's Wife* (1915), 34.

11. Kleinegger (1987).

12. Ward (1920), from a survey of 10,044 farm women conducted in 1919 by the USDA.

13. Ciancanelli, pp. 112-114, proposes a "probable rate" of participation that includes *all* farm wives, and a "minimum rate" (42.1 percent) that is based on a 1964 study by the Department of Agriculture.

14. Doran (1775).

15. Boydston (1990).

16. Ibid.

17. Tyron (1917).

18. Boydston (1990).

19. Pinchbeck (1930).

20. *The New York Journal* (Jan. 21, 1893), quoted in Matthaei (1982).

21. The occupation of the wife is assumed to be related to her family's business if it is listed in the PUMS as being within the same industry as the husband's.

22. Edwards, Reich, and Weisskopf (1978).

23. A. Carter (1970).

24. Ciancanelli (1983).

25. See Appendix A for a description of these categories.

26. Inferred from above results and the PUMS from 1940 to 1990.

27. See Carter and Sutch (1996, Appendix A) for a discussion of some criticisms and a verification of the self-employment data contained in the 1910

PUMS.

28. Carter and Sutch (1996, Appendix A).
29. Ibid.
30. Ibid.

CHAPTER IV

Explaining the Racial Gap in Married Women's Labor Force Participation

The results of Chapter III bring to light two important facts: that the recorded participation rate of married women differed drastically by race around the turn of the century and that rates of male self-employment did as well. These findings, taken together, may provide the answer to a question that has eluded labor economists for decades. That is, what is the *reason* for the large and unexplained racial gap in married women's labor force participation before 1940? In this chapter, I propose that the answer to this question lies in the discovery of a large number of white women who were left out of census employment statistics when in fact they performed work for their self-employed husbands. I investigate this possibility in detail by examining the racial components of the labor supply decision.

RACIAL DIFFERENCES IN MARRIED WOMEN'S PROPENSITY TO PARTICIPATE

As can be seen in Table 4.1, the labor force participation rate of women in the United States has indeed been marked by substantial differences by race and marital status. The rate of participation for white women has been recorded as increasing dramatically over the past century, while that for black women has remained fairly constant. Census data indicate that between 1880 and 1990, the labor force participation rate for white women rose from 13.5 percent to 55.7 percent and that for black women, the increase was from 44.0 percent to 56.9 percent. The most dramatic gains during this period came from the ten-fold increase recorded for married white women.

The difference in the propensities of black and white married women to work, however, is not at all surprising given what we know about the lower labor income and higher unemployment of black husbands, higher black male mortality, and higher rates of female-headed households. Black men were more likely to participate in the labor market than white men around the turn of the century. In 1880, census figures indicate that only 4.8 percent of all black males over 14 years old stated that they were not working, whereas 8.5 percent of white males declared no occupation. Black men, however, were subject to more unemployment (on average 3 weeks per year as compared to 1.6 weeks for whites who listed an occupation). Black men also had lower paying occupations than whites.[1] They were abundantly represented in the unskilled categories, but few appear in professional occupations.

What is rather puzzling, however, is the fact that even when these disparities in the experiences of black and white women are controlled for, there remains a sizable unexplained gap in participation, indicating that if black and white women had *identical* characteristics, black women would, for unobservable reasons, still supply more labor.[2]

PREVIOUS EFFORTS TO EXPLAIN THE GAP

Goldin (1977) explores the labor market characteristics of a random sample of women drawn from seven southern cities in the U.S. during the census years 1870 and 1880 and employs a probit model to analyze the extent to which certain personal, household, and labor market characteristics affect the probability of a particular woman choosing to supply labor outside her home.[3] She recognizes, however, that data constraints have prevented a thorough comparison of the historical nature of these racial differences with the current period.

Goldin's explanation of the unexplained portion of the gap emphasizes the effects of slavery in creating differences between black and white women in their propensity to work. Other authors have offered such explanations as differences in family life cycles and quality of education, discrimination in housing and labor markets, and measurement problems in valuing part-time labor. Because no study to date has been able to reduce the unexplained portion of the racial gap in participation to less than 30 percent, we are left with a need to explain a large part of the participation gap in other terms.[4]

This chapter extends Goldin's analysis in three ways. First, economic and demographic variables are examined over a longer period of time—1880 through 1990.[5] Second, characteristics are analyzed for the U.S. as a whole, rather than the seven southern cities in Goldin's analysis. Goldin restricts her analysis to the South since, in both 1870 and 1880, over 90% of all blacks lived there. She focuses attention on cities because, as she says, ". . . such data allow a richer analysis than those for rural areas". It is not clear why this is the case, since in 1870 only 8.8% of all southern blacks lived in cities. Furthermore, most farmers were both self-employed and in rural areas. There is a long-standing recognition of the importance of wives to the market output of their farmer husbands yet, as was shown in Chapter III, an extremely small percentage of such women were recorded as participating in the labor market. Since this effect is less significant for the wives of self-employed urban men, Goldin completely misses the effect of this potential undercounting of married women's work by concentrating on cities.[6]

Finally, and most importantly, this chapter adapts Goldin's model to include an examination of women's participation in family businesses. As will be shown, the incorporation of this self-employment component is the necessary step in providing an explanation for the racial gap in married women's labor force participation.

THE LINK BETWEEN SELF-EMPLOYMENT AND PARTICIPATION

The objective of this chapter is to examine the labor force experience of black and white women from 1880 through 1990 both to extend our historical knowledge of this subject and to develop an explanation for the long-run differences between these two groups. I demonstrate that this explanation can be found by examining the link between married women's labor supply around the turn of the century and their husband's self-employment status, which also differs substantially by race.

The link between married women's labor supply and self-employment may answer two questions that have, until now, been considered only separately. Those are (a) why black married women have historically been recorded as participating more actively in the paid labor force and (b) why black men do not become self-employed to the same extent as other men [Fairlie and Meyer (1996)]. It must be emphasized that it is the *link* between these two questions that is of concern in this book, rather than the answers to the questions separately.

THE CHARACTERISTICS OF WOMEN IN THIS SAMPLE

The variables suggested by previous labor force studies to analyze the participation of married black and white women include both economic characteristics, such as family wealth and occupations, and demographic data, such as the woman's age, her family size and her household's composition. These variables are described below for the individuals in this sample (the PUMS).[7]

ECONOMIC VARIABLES

Table 4.1 shows female labor force participation by race, marital status, and age for each of the years under study. This table indicates the noted rise in recorded participation rates of white married women over the century. As is clearly evident, black married women have been recorded as participating in the labor force at much higher rates than married white women. An interesting change in trend, however, exists among the other marital categories (single, divorced, widowed, etc.). Before 1980, black women supplied more labor than white women across all age groups and marital categories. Beginning in 1980, white women supplied more labor than black women across all age groups, except over 65, and across all marital categories, except married.

From Census data we can see that the overall rate of male self-employment was decreasing each year until at least 1980 as farming (a main component of self-employment) became less common. However, this trend has recently begun to change as self-employment rates have increased fairly substantially, especially for white males between 1980 and 1990. Table 3.1 illustrates the fact that white men have historically been far more likely to engage in self-employment than black men; a difference that has increased over time.

DEMOGRAPHIC VARIABLES

Table 4.2 presents the age distribution for the females in this sample relative to that of males. Table 4.3 shows the marital status of the women, age 15 and over, relative to men by race for each year. Black and white women were equally represented across marital categories until around 1980 at which time a much larger fraction of black women in the single category and a much smaller fraction in the married category emerged, relative to white women. Indeed, in 1980 the percentage of all black women who were single was 43.8, while for white women this percentage was 37.0 and the percentage of black women who were married was 24.7, compared to a rate of 44.9 percent for white women. In 1990, 41.3 percent of black women were single and 22.1 percent were married, while 33.8 percent of white women were single and 45.4 percent were married.

Finally, Goldin (1990) finds that from 1880 to 1910, the percentage of black families with children which were headed by a female was identical to that for whites. Approximately 30 percent of all two-parent and female-parent families with at least one child were headed by a female, both for blacks and whites. She also finds, for the same period, that black families were smaller on average than were white families—there were an average of 1.78 black children per two-parent family, but 2.31 white children over this time period.

THE RACIAL GAP IN MARRIED WOMEN'S LABOR FORCE PARTICIPATION

Of direct interest for this chapter is the fact that in 1880, black women's labor force participation rate was 26.9 points higher than white women's, in 1900 it was 19.8 points higher, and in 1910, it was an astounding 45.0 points higher.[8]

Obviously, some portion of this gap can be attributed to differences in the characteristics of black and white women, while some portion of the gap cannot be explained by these differences. It is this unexplained part of the participation gap that many previous studies have attempted to reduce.[9] Goldin, for example, finds that black women supply abundantly more labor than white women, but she is unable to explain over 30 percent of the gap in black and white married women's labor force participation. No study to date has considered the effects of husband's self-employment on the unexplained portion of the gap.

The aggregate estimates of married women's labor supply obtained from census documents hide important differences in the effects of self-employment within racial groups. A few calculations demonstrate the magnitude of these differences. In Chapter II we noted that adding to the count of women in the labor force all those with self-employed husbands (but nonetheless counted as *not* gainfully occupied by census enumerators) causes the overall gap in participation between black and white married women to decline significantly. This exercise indicates that it is possible that an enormous number of white married women were excluded from the count of gainfully occupied—most likely due to the inability of census enumerators to recognize the hidden work that some of these women performed in their families' businesses. This was less likely to be the case for black women who were less likely to live in families with a self-employed male and, hence, tended to work in more visible jobs.

EMPIRICAL ESTIMATION

In this section, I analyze the effect of considering self-employment on the unexplained portion of the black/white participation gap. To this end, probit estimation is used to estimate an adapted version of Mincer's (1966) model of married women's labor supply, expressed as:[10]

$$m_i^b = \beta_0^b + \sum_i \beta_j^b X_{ji}^b + u_i^b \tag{1}$$

$$m_i^w = \beta_0^w + \sum_i \beta_j^w X_{ji}^w + u_i^w \tag{2}$$

where the superscripts b and w denote the equations for black and white married women; m is a dichotomous variable taking on the value one if the woman has a gainful occupation, zero otherwise; and X_{ji} is a vector of personal and household variables for woman i. The independent variables to be used in this equation are: five categorical variables identifying the woman's age group; four categorical variables identifying the geographical region in which the woman lived and one describing her urban/rural status; a discrete variable representing the number of months the husband was unemployed during the previous year; and six dichotomous variables: the woman's health status,[11] the presence of at least one child under the age of five, whether the woman is foreign or native born, the presence of boarders in the household, the presence of servants employed by the household head, and whether the household owns or rents their home.[12]

The last three dummy variables—presence of boarders, presence of servants, and home-ownership, serve as proxies for family income and wealth since there are two problems with using more direct measures of income. The more practical reason is that direct income measures are simply not available in the PUMS. The second reason, as discussed in Woodman (1977), is that the commonly used method of imputing family income can be shown to be erroneous. This method, used in Goldin (1977), calculates family income by multiplying average wage rates for the husband's stated occupation by twelve months and then deducting the number of months the husband was unemployed. The problem with this method is the assumption that wage rates for the same jobs were equal for both black and white men. Higgs (1975) asserted that there was little racial discrimination in wage payments *when the jobs and output were identical* and that if a white worker was for any reason more productive than a black worker in the same job, the differences in pay merely reflected differences in the value of the output of each worker. However, even if this argument is accepted it does not wholly support using the method described above to calculate family income since the job categories in the census are too broad to differentiate between levels of skill, exact work performed, and the value of output. Given these significant chances for error, variables measuring home-ownership, boarders, and servants will be used as proxies for family wealth and income in this analysis.

In order to decipher the effect of male self-employment on the racial gap in married women's participation, it is necessary to use the Blinder(1973)/Oaxaca (1973) decomposition method of distinguishing between the explained and unexplained portions of the racial participation gap.[13] The total gap in participation, *TGAP*, canbe derived by subtracting equation(1) from equation (2) to arrive at the following:

$$TGAP = m_i^b - m_i^w = b_0^b + \sum_i b_i^b \overline{X}_i^b - \left(b_0^w + \sum_i b_i^w \overline{X}_i^w \right) \quad (3)$$

This difference in the participation rates of black and white married women can now be decomposed into explained and unexplained portions. To calculate the portion of the gap explained by differences in characteristics, we estimate the participation rate that white (black) women would have if they had the black (white) sample characteristics. That is, using black women as the reference group, we can define the explained portion, *EXP*, as:[14]

$$EXP = \sum_i \beta_i^b (\overline{X}_i^b - \overline{X}_i^w)$$

(4)

The unexplained portion of the gap, *UNEXP*, (again using black women as the reference group) is calculated as the change in participation that results if the probability of participation is determined by the white probit coefficients. In other words, it is the portion that reflects differences in the effects a given characteristic has on black and white women's decision to participate in the labor force. This is the portion that I attempt to reduce. It is constructed as

$$UNEXP = \beta_0^b - \beta_0^w + \sum_i \overline{X}_i^w (\beta_i^b - \beta_i^w)$$

(5)

As defined above, *EXP* represents the gap in participation explained by racial differences in observed characteristics and *UNEXP* captures differences in the probability of participation due to unobservable characteristics such as racial discrimination or differences in the social acceptability of working outside the home.

The portion of *EXP* that is due to differences in the *r*th explanatory variable is defined as:

$$EXP_r = EXP \left[\frac{(\overline{X}_r^b - \overline{X}_r^w)\beta_r^b}{(\overline{X}^b - \overline{X}^w)\beta^b} \right]$$

Twelve probit regressions were estimated in all (four each in 1880, 1900, and 1910) in order to analyze the effects of self-employment on the unexplained gap in participation. For each year, two equations were estimated for the black sample and two for the white sample. The first equation for each group included all of the independent variables identified at the beginning of this section and the second equation was an augmented version of equations (1) and (2) which included a dichotomous variable (S_i) indicating whether a particular woman's husband was self-employed.

RESULTS AND IMPLICATIONS

Tables 4.4 through 4.6 present the results of the twelve probit regressions described above. As can be seen, all variables have the expected signs and nearly all are significant. Equations (1) and (2) describe the determinants of recorded labor force participation for black and white women, exclusive of their husbands' self-employment status. In each year, women living in the North, East, and especially the South are more likely to have been recorded as gainfully occupied than women living in the West. Women in urban areas are more likely to have been recorded with an occupation than are women in rural areas, as are women whose husbands have experienced a spell of unemployment during the previous year and foreign-born women. Women in poor health, with children under age five, with boarders, or with servants are less likely to have been recorded as gainfully occupied.

Equations (3) and (4) describe the determinants of labor force participation for black and white women, including the dummy variable representing their husbands' self-employment status. As can be seen, the explanatory power of the models increase with the inclusion of the self-employment indicator, as does the percentage predicted correctly for each equation, especially for the white wives. None of the coefficients experience a change in sign, although most are reduced in size due to the fact that the self-employment variable has acquired much of the explanatory power in the model.

The negative sign on this variable indicates that a woman was *less* likely to be counted as gainfully occupied if her husband was self-employed. This surprising finding confirms the suspicion that such women, while generally performing work of the GNP-type in her family's business (and therefore less likely to be working for pay outside the home), were not counted as such by census enumerators. Note that the coefficient on the self-employment indicator variable in the equation for white wives is larger than that in the black wives equation. This implies that enumerators were less likely to count white women as employed than black women, even if they were both working in family businesses.

The top part of Tables 4.7 through 4.9 present the decompositions of the total participation gap (26.9 percent in 1880, 19.8 percent in 1900, and 45.0 percent in 1910)[15] into explained and unexplained components when husband's self-employment status is not considered. The decompositions indicate the change in participation that the reference group would realize if the characteristics or probit coefficients were switched to the comparison group's. Using the white wives as the reference group, labor market characteristics are responsible for 56.2 percent, 46.7 percent, and 42.7 percent of the 1880, 1900, and 1910 gaps in participation. Using the black wives as the reference group, the explained portions rise to 66.7 percent, 69.1 percent, and 66.8 percent since weighting by black characteristics accentuates the racial differences in the probability of participation (probit coefficients). These results are comparable to those in the literature on the racial participation gap mentioned above, which do not consider self-employment.

The middle part of each table presents the same decompositions when husband's self-employment status *is* considered. As can be seen, the unexplained portion of the total gap in participation is reduced with the inclusion of the self-employment indicator variable. Using white wives as the reference group, the explained portion rises to 91.1 percent, 88.7 percent, and 84.2 percent of the 1880, 1900, and 1910 racial gap in participation. Thus, by accounting for husband's self-employment status in the probability of women's participation, we are left with only a small fraction of the total racial gap to be explained in other terms. Recall that Goldin (1977) was able to explain only about 70 percent of the racial participation gap and that other studies (mentioned in footnote 2) have explained even less.[16]

The bottom part of the tables list the explanatory power of each independent variable using both white and black probit coefficients. The most striking result is that, in each year, husband's self-employment status has significant power in explaining the gap in married women's participation rates by race, especially when we use white wives as the reference group. It is not surprising, therefore, that the studies referred to in footnote 2, which did not consider the effects of self-employment, were unable to reduce the unexplainable portion of the total gap to as great a degree and had to rely on ad hoc explanations for the remaining gap, such as indirect legacies of slavery, education quality differences, and marital instability in black families.

The explanations offered by previous authors certainly had some effect on the racial gap in married women's labor force participation. However, to attribute over 30 percent of the gap to such factors seems unreasonable. This chapter improves our current understanding of the racial participation gap by providing a concrete explanation for it— unrecorded participation in a family business that differed by race.

This understanding has implications for the U-shaped pattern of married women's labor force participation discussed in Chapter III. With the revised estimates of married women's GNP-producing activities, a new pattern of participation emerged that was different from the traditional U-shape story around the turn of the century. It is important to keep in mind, however, that the results obtained in Chapter III were *underestimates* of married women's true contributions to GNP. Therefore, the revised pattern of participation, as was indicated in Figure 3.2, is biased toward implying that the rate at which married women's were involved in GNP-production did not change much over the course of the century. In fact, we know that the true pattern of married women's participation was marked by higher rates around the turn of the century than those indicated in Chapter III due to the fact that not *all* of the occupations in which men were self-employed were captured.

With the insights of the current chapter, we realize that the majority of these "left-out" women were the wives of white, self-employed men. In other words, it was the hidden work of women in family businesses—who tended to be white—that was most often overlooked by census enumerators. This type of underenumeration was a major cause of the racial participation gap puzzle that has eluded economists for decades.

The results in this chapter provide a clear explanation for the previously unexplainable portion of the gap from 1880 to 1910. However, because self-employment was not a significant determinant of married women's labor supply in the post-1940 period, an analysis of this data is left for future research.

Table 4.1: Female Labor Force Participation Rates by Marital Status, Race, and Nativity (as Recorded by Census Enumerators), 1880-1990

	> 16 Years Old		> 15		> 16	
	1880	*1900*	*1910[a]*	*1940*	*1980*	*1990*
Total	17.0	21.8	25.8	26.9	50.1	56.0
Married	4.6	5.3	10.7	13.4	49.3	57.7
Single	37.6	48.0	54.5	54.8	60.1	67.0
White	13.5	19.1	22.0	25.6	49.6	55.7
Married	1.7	3.4	6.3	12.4	48.4	57.1
Single	34.4	45.9	52.7	54.9	62.6	68.6
Black	44.0	41.8	55.8	38.7	51.2	56.9
Married	28.2	22.1	34.3	24.6	59.3	66.0
Single	65.2	66.5	73.4	49.8	41.2	55.3
Nonwhite	41.7	43.4	61.4	38.9	53.1	57.6
Married	26.2	26.0	51.3	24.2	58.2	62.2
Single	64.0	65.1	75.7	53.7	49.8	60.1
Foreign	17.6	20.8	22.4	19.2	42.4	53.2
Married	2.7	4.0	7.3	11.8	45.3	54.9
Single	65.1	72.0	78.2	63.0	54.8	61.4

[a] As reported by census enumerators, the figures for 1910 are not directly comparable with the other years due to the well-documented "overcount" of agricultural workers, particularly women, in this year. See Chapter II for a thorough discussion.

Married includes married, spouse present and married, spouse absent in 1880, 1900, 1910; includes married, spouse present in 1940, 1980, 1990. Single includes single and unknown in 1880, 1900, 1910; includes single only in 1940, 1980, 1990.

Table 4.2: Age Distribution by Race and Sex for the U.S., 1880-1990

Age	Black		White	
1880	*Female*	*Male*	*Female*	*Male*
15-19	17.5	17.6	16.5	15.3
20-29	31.9	31.4	29.1	29.1
30-39	19.6	18.7	20.3	20.9
40-49	14.0	13.4	14.9	14.7
50-64	11.7	13.7	13.3	14.2
over 64	5.4	5.3	5.9	5.8
Sample	15,509	15,113	133,278	139,447
1900				
15-19	19.6	18.4	15.0	14.4
20-29	32.2	32.4	28.5	26.7
30-39	19.3	17.4	21.1	22.1
40-49	13.0	13.2	14.8	16.6
50-64	11.1	13.1	14.0	13.9
over 64	4.9	5.4	6.7	6.2
Sample	3,312	3,246	27,331	28,972
1910				
15-19	17.6	16.2	15.0	13.8
20-29	32.2	29.4	27.3	27.0
30-39	21.4	21.8	21.2	21.7
40-49	13.1	14.2	15.5	16.2
50-64	11.2	13.2	14.2	15.1
over 64	4.6	5.2	6.8	6.2
Sample	9,513	9,707	106,324	115,180

Table 4.2: Age Distribution by Race and Sex for the U.S., 1880-1990 (continued)

Age	Black		White	
1940	Female	Male	Female	Male
15-19	15.5	15.7	12.6	12.5
20-29	26.0	24.3	23.0	22.6
30-39	23.4	21.2	20.1	19.2
40-49	16.5	17.1	17.0	17.9
50-64	12.4	14.9	17.8	18.9
over 64	6.2	6.8	9.6	9.0
Sample	4,822	4,497	45,113	45,342
1980				
15-19	15.6	17.8	11.0	12.3
20-29	25.7	26.7	21.7	23.4
30-39	17.9	17.7	17.3	18.5
40-49	13.1	12.9	12.7	13.4
50-64	16.0	15.3	20.0	19.6
over 64	11.7	9.6	17.3	12.8
Sample	10,177	8,597	79,334	72,762
1990				
15-19	11.5	14.1	7.9	9.0
20-29	21.0	23.4	17.6	19.1
30-39	22.6	21.3	20.0	21.6
40-49	15.2	16.1	16.0	16.9
50-64	15.6	14.5	17.9	18.1
over 64	14.2	10.6	20.6	15.3
Sample	10,255	8,467	85,030	77,978

Table 4.3: Marital Status by Sex and Race, Age 15 and Over for the U.S., 1880-1990

	Single		Married		Other	
	White	*Black*	*White*	*Black*	*White*	*Black*
1880						
Female	55.8	57.6	35.0	29.4	9.2	13.0
Male	60.9	62.9	33.6	30.2	5.4	6.9
No. of	118700	15885	74517	8096	19525	3593
obs.	135106)	(17494)	(74521)	(8396)	(12067)	(1918)
1900						
Female	54.4	57.5	36.2	29.7	9.4	12.8
Male	60.0	63.3	34.6	30.3	5.5	6.4
No. of	22749	3186	15165	1647	3923	711
obs.	(26318)	(3441)	(15168)	(1649)	(2406)	(350)
1910						
Female	52.7	54.3	39.8	35.1	7.5	10.6
Male	58.4	59.5	38.2	36.4	3.4	4.2
No. of	82504	8320	62272	5374	11689	1622
obs.	(97310)	(9205)	(63645)	(5628)	(5669)	(643)
1940						
Female	44.5	48.3	43.8	33.5	11.8	18.1
Male	50.2	55.6	43.4	35.4	6.5	9.0
No. of	26767	3394	26313	2354	7068	1274
obs.	(30451)	(3684)	(26318)	(2350)	(3912)	(598)
1980						
Female	37.0	43.8	44.9	24.7	18.1	31.6
Male	44.4	58.6	47.7	28.6	7.9	12.9
No. of	36985	6168	44938	3475	18127	4454
obs.	(41951)	(7291)	(44989)	(3555)	(7472)	(1606)
1990						
Female	33.8	41.3	45.4	22.1	20.8	36.6
Male	42.3	59.7	48.2	26.2	9.5	14.2
No. of	35720	5748	47926	3071	21950	5111
obs.	(42177)	(7215)	(48106)	(3165)	(9480)	(1711)

Table 4.4: Probit Coefficients and Summary Statistics (Dependent Variable: Labor Force Status), 1880

	w/o Self-Employment		w/Self-Employment	
	(1)	(2)	(3)	(4)
	Blk wives	Wht wives	Blk wives	Wht wives
Constant	-.92	-1.01	-1.07	-.96
Age 15-24	.26*	.17*	.23*	.16*
25-29	.15*	.08	.11*	.05
30-34	.43*	.32*	.29*	.20*
35-39	.19*	.11*	.13*	.07*
40-49 [a]	.12	.06	.09	.04`
North	.39*	.26*	.33*	.21*
South	.97*	.82*	.91*	.70*
East [b]	.24*	.20*	.19*	.14*
Urban	.84*	.79*	.77*	.66*
Husband unempld	1.14*	1.03*	1.09*	.95*
Poor health	-.49	-.62*	-.41	-.57*
Children < 5 years	-.41*	-.36*	-.37*	-.25*
Foreign	.12*	.19*	.10*	.17*
Boarders	-.23*	-.36*	-.19*	-.33*
Servants	-.26	-.56*	-.22	-.54*
Owns home [c]	—	—	—	—
Husband self-empld	—	—	-1.27*	-2.88*
-2 x LLR [d]	137.6	142.9	157.8	162.4
% predicted correctly	86.2	89.7	94.3	98.8

* Significant at the 95 percent level.
[a] Age 50 and over is the omitted category.
[b] West is the omitted category.
[c] Information on home ownership is not available in the 1880 PUMS.
[d] Minus two times the log likelihood ratio, which has the chi-squared distribution with 14 degrees of freedom for equations (1) and (2) and 15 for (3) and (4). The null hypothesis is that all coefficients are zero.

**Table 4.5: Probit Coefficients and Summary Statistics
(Dependent Variable: Labor Force Status), 1900**

	w/o Self-Employment		w/Self-Employment	
	(1)	(2)	(3)	(4)
	Blk wives	Wht wives	Blk wives	Wht wives
Constant	-.87	-1.14	-1.11	-1.03
Age 15-24	.26*	.19*	.24*	.17*
25-29	.21*	.12*	.16*	.08
30-34	.49*	.41*	.31*	.29*
35-39	.27*	.21*	.20*	.16*
40-49 [a]	.15	.09	.12*	.05
North	.45*	.21*	.39*	.16*
South	1.02*	.96*	.97*	.89*
East [b]	.27*	.22*	.24*	.16*
Urban	.94*	.86*	.82*	.78*
Husband unempld	1.06*	.99*	1.00*	.91*
Poor health	-.36*	-.57*	-.30	-.48*
Children < 5 years	-.40*	-.29*	-.31*	-.24*
Foreign	.17*	.22*	.13*	.20*
Boarders	-.26*	-.32*	-.21*	-.29*
Servants	-.18	-.29	-.15	-.24
Owns home	-.46*	-.52*	-.39*	-.47*
Husband self-empld	—	—	-1.16*	-2.69*
-2 x LLR [c]	142.8	150.7	148.0	159.4
% predicted correctly	84.3	88.1	90.7	96.2

* Significant at the 95 percent level.

[a] Age 50 and over is the omitted category.

[b] West is the omitted category.

[c] Minus two times the log likelihood ratio, which has the chi-squared distribution with 14 degrees of freedom for equations (1) and (2) and 15 for (3) and (4). The null hypothesis is that all coefficients are zero.

**Table 4.6: Probit Coefficients and Summary Statistics
(Dependent Variable: Labor Force Status), 1910**

	w/o Self-Employment		w/Self-Employment	
	(1)	(2)	(3)	(4)
	Blk wives	Wht wives	Blk wives	Wht wives
Constant	-1.21	-1.30	-1.29	-1.36
Age 15-24	.37*	.21*	.35*	.17*
25-29	.38*	.19*	.31*	.16*
30-34	.52*	.49*	.46*	.34*
35-39	.33*	.30*	.27*	.25*
40-49 [a]	.26*	.20	.18	.14
North	.62*	.48*	.57*	.41*
South	1.39	1.22*	1.28*	1.09*
East [b]	.41*	.33*	.37*	.28*
Urban	1.20*	1.06*	1.11*	.94*
Husband unempld	1.51*	1.42*	1.32*	1.29*
Poor health	-.41*	-.49*	-.36	-.38
Children < 5 years	-.56*	-.40*	-.51*	-.36*
Foreign	.22*	.41*	.16*	.34*
Boarders	-.30*	-.33*	-.21*	-.26*
Servants	-.24	-.37	-.18	-.24
Owns home	-.67*	-.73*	-.52*	-.60*
Husband self-empld	—	—	-1.68*	-3.03*
-2 x LLR [c]	128.7	141.9	138.0	160.5
% predicted correctly	85.8	89.7	91.3	97.6

* Significant at the 95 percent level.
[a] Age 50 and over is the omitted category.
[b] West is the omitted category.
[c] Minus two times the log likelihood ratio, which has the chi-squared distribution with 14 degrees of freedom for equations (1) and (2) and 15 for (3) and (4). The null hypothesis is that all coefficients are zero.

Table 4.7: Decomposition of the Racial Participation Gap for Married Women, 1880

	Without Self-Employment Variable	
	White Wives	Black Wives
Due to characteristics	11.6%	17.9%
Due to coefficients	15.3	9.0
Total gap	26.9%	26.9%

	With Self-Employment Variable	
	White Wives	Black Wives
Due to characteristics	24.5%	23.1%
Due to coefficients	2.4	3.8
Total gap	26.9%	26.9%

Explanatory Power of Observed Characteristics

	w/o Self-Employment		w/Self-Employment	
Reference group	Blk wives	Wht wives	Blk wives	Wht wives
Total explained	17.9%	11.6%	23.1%	24.5%
Portion explained by:				
Age	0.23	0.14	0.21	0.12
North	0.62	0.30	0.35	0.28
South	0.93	0.36	0.74	0.34
East	0.29	0.21	0.18	0.20
Urban	1.68	1.05	1.07	0.99
Mos. hus unemp	7.29	4.62	6.16	4.60
Health status	0.51	-0.29	0.44	-0.11
Children < 5 yrs.	3.03	1.99	2.76	1.94
Foreign-born	1.62	2.13	1.34	2.06
Boarders in hhld	1.74	1.17	1.01	1.12
Employs servants	-0.04	-0.08	-0.02	-0.06
Husband self-empld	—	—	8.89	12.94

Table 4.8: Decomposition of the Racial Participation Gap for Married Women, 1900

Without Self-Employment Variable

	White Wives	Black Wives
Due to characteristics	9.2%	13.7%
Due to coefficients	10.6	6.1
Total gap	19.8%	19.8%

With Self-Employment Variable

	White Wives	Black Wives
Due to characteristics	17.6%	14.4%
Due to coefficients	2.2	5.4
Total gap	19.8%	19.8%

Explanatory Power of Observed Characteristics

	w/o Self-Employment		w/Self-Employment	
Reference group	Blk wives	Wht wives	Blk wives	Wht wives
Total explained	13.7%	9.2%	14.4%	17.6%

Portion explained by:

Age	0.24	0.13	0.21	0.12
North	0.53	0.21	0.22	0.16
South	0.91	0.41	0.66	0.35
East	0.21	0.10	0.13	0.08
Urban	1.22	0.96	0.79	0.72
Mos. hus unemp	5.17	2.19	3.09	1.78
Health status	-0.17	-0.28	-0.20	-0.22
Children < 5 yrs.	2.00	2.26	1.24	1.51
Foreign-born	1.29	1.53	0.70	1.44
Boarders in hhld	1.31	1.21	0.65	0.48
Employs servants	-0.06	-0.10	-0.05	-0.09
Husband self-empld	—	—	6.13	10.12

Table 4.9: Decomposition of the Racial Participation Gap for Married Women, 1910

Without Self-Employment Variable

	White Wives	Black Wives
Due to characteristics	25.3%	30.1%
Due to coefficients	19.7	14.9
Total gap	45.0%	45.0%

With Self-Employment Variable

	White Wives	Black Wives
Due to characteristics	37.9%	32.0%
Due to coefficients	7.1	13.0
Total gap	45.0%	45.0%

Explanatory Power of Observed Characteristics

	w/o Self-Employment		w/Self-Employment	
Reference group	Blk wives	Wht wives	Blk wives	Wht wives
Total explained	30.1%	25.3%	32.0%	37.9%
Portion explained by				
Age	2.08	1.64	1.94	1.62
North	2.28	1.57	2.04	1.51
South	4.27	3.03	4.11	2.93
East	1.44	0.94	1.32	0.81
Urban	3.13	2.36	2.30	2.34
Mos. hus unemp	7.24	5.90	6.12	5.83
Health status	1.39	1.28	1.35	1.06
Children < 5 yrs.	3.05	2.62	2.27	2.59
Foreign-born	2.09	2.49	1.71	2.36
Boarders in hhld	2.62	2.05	1.84	2.00
Employs servants	-0.13	-0.15	-0.09	-0.10
Husband self-empld	—	—	6.06	13.48

NOTES

1. Goldin (1977), pp. 96-98.

2. For discussions see Goldin (1977), Bowen and Finegan (1969), Cain (1966), Sweet (1973), Bell (1974), and Hall (1973).

3. The seven southern cities analyzed in Goldin's study are Atlanta, Charleston, Mobile, New Orleans, Norfolk, Richmond, and Savannah.

4. See references in footnote 2.

5. Descriptive statistics are presented for the years 1880 through 1990. However, because it was shown in Chapter III that self-employment was a significant determinant of a women's labor force status only through 1910, the empirical section will focus on the years 1880 through 1910.

6. Goldin (1989) uses the 1910 estimates of farm wives' participation in the labor market as an upper bound. See Chapter II for a discussion.

7. The PUMS is described in detail in Chapter III.

8. Both the absolute size of the gap as well as the unexplained portion in married women's labor force participation during the post-1940 period is significantly smaller and, therefore, less of a theoretical puzzle [see Table 4.1 and Lehrer (1988), Bowen and Finegan (1972), and Cain (1966)].

9. Goldin (1977) arrives at an adjusted participation rate for black married women in the South of 33 percentage points higher than white married women in 1880, a difference which is even larger than the unadjusted gap of 26.91 points. See also the studies mentioned in footnote 2.

10. A Chow test revealed that the hypothesis of no structural differences between models of black and white married women's labor force participation could be rejected at any level of significance. The equations are, therefore, estimated separately.

11. This variable takes on the value one if the woman is listed in the census as being blind, deaf, idiotic, insane, disabled, or having a disease on the day of enumeration and is available in 1880 only.

12. These income-related variables have been constructed such that they do not attribute the wealth of the household to boarders or servants of the household. Questions about home ownership were not asked in the 1880 census and are therefore not included in the 1880 regressions.

13. See Oaxaca and Ransom (1994) for extensions.

14. A symmetric equation results from using the white women as the reference group.

15. Refer to Table 4.1.

16. Replicating Goldin's (1977) results using her restricted sample of

seven southern cities causes the explained portion of the racial participation gap to rise to 89.7 percent, 87.1 percent, and 83.0 percent in 1880, 1900, and 1910, respectively. Recall that in her study, Goldin is able to explain only about 70 percent of the gap in 1880 (1900 and 1910 are not analyzed). Hence, we can conclude that the presence of a self-employed male in a woman's household was as important in determining her recorded labor force status in the urban South as it was for the U.S. as a whole.

CHAPTER V

Conclusions, Implications, and Extensions

This book describes the underestimation of the female labor force and provides more accurate estimates of the actual contributions of married women to GNP in the United States from 1880 to 1940.

Using data from the Public Use Microdata Samples (PUMS), I have demonstrated that a substantial number of women were left out of the census count of gainfully occupied persons in 1880, 1900, and 1910. This undercount was in part due to enumerator neglect, but was most significantly attributable to the fact that many women performing work in family-run businesses were overlooked, despite the fact that this work was of the type considered gainful by census definitions of employment. The traditionally-accepted pattern of initial decreases in labor force participation followed by rapid increases over the century is replaced by one of high rates across years. It is shown that women were producing for the market before the modernizing structural changes had occurred and remained productive long afterward. The work rates estimated for women in the United States in the critical period of 1880 to 1910 are as high or higher than those reported in the post-World War II decades. Women were evidently not "pushed" out of the labor force by industrialization. Instead, they were integrated as unpaid and largely unreported family laborers.

This book also shows that there exists a crucial link between the labor force participation of married women at the turn of the century and their husband's self-employment status. My results indicate that a significant number of white, married women were performing work at home in family businesses of the type that was considered gainful by census definitions of employment but were, nonetheless, not counted as gainfully occupied by census enumerators. Controlling for this phenomenon in probit regressions of black and white married women's labor force participation significantly reduces the size of the previously unexplainable gap in participation by race.

IMPLICATIONS OF FINDINGS

It has been argued that married women constitute a "hidden" labor force in economies whose industrial structure is characterized by a large number of small, family-based production units.[1] Because their market work is unpaid and because it is performed alongside their family obligations, their connection to the labor force is obscured. It was the case in the United States before 1940 that the primary production unit was family-based. In 1900, I estimate that 32.3 percent of all married women contributed to GNP, many in family businesses. The total *reported* employment of married women was only 5.3 percent. Thus, the "hidden" labor force was over five times the size of the reported labor force. By 1940, nearly all women working or seeking work were reported as members of the labor force. This was due to two factors: (a) changes in census definitions of employment that were more inclusive of women's work, and (b) the shift from employment in family businesses to more easily counted employment as wage workers outside the home that married women experiences over the course of the century. This book makes possible the identification of this hidden labor of women. It provides much needed clarification of the characteristics of market production, permitting empirical estimation of women's work in economies undergoing structural transformation, as was the United States around the turn of the century.

As noted by Goldin (1994), both the United States from 1880 to 1940 and many developing countries today report very low levels of labor force participation for married women. The labor force segment seemingly most affected by modernization processes appears to be single women. The standard theory holds that they work for wages outside the home prior to marriage and withdraw from the labor force once married. The empirical research of this book documents the continuation of market work by these married women only as unreported workers in home-based production. Married women in such circumstances constitute a "hidden" labor force.

This "hidden" labor force obscures many issues. In particular, it calls into question the accuracy of estimates of U.S. productivity growth over the twentieth century. As discussed in Chapter I, including all married women who performed GNP-type work on family farms from 1880 to 1900 would increase the size of the agricultural work force even more dramatically than Geib-Gundersen and Zahrt's (1996) estimates that consider only farm laborers counted but misclassified as nonfarm laborers. Thus, agricultural productivity over this period may indeed have been even *lower* than their already lower estimates and industrial productivity even higher.

The "hidden" labor of women also obscures the results of the transition by married women from home production (of the GNP-type) to the wage labor force. This transition most likely affected the very institution of self-employment and, thus, provides an answer to Carter and Sutch's (1996) question about the decline in self-employment over the course of the twentieth century. As opportunities increased in the wage labor force for such women, many were induced to leave their careers in family enterprises for the high-paying jobs outside the home. This book illustrates that it was likely the case that these women played such crucial roles in the operation of family businesses that their entry into paid labor resulted in the demise of the profitability of self-employment for many families.

EXTENSIONS

With the insights of this book, we realize that the majority of the women left out of census employment statistics were the wives of white, self-employed men. In other words, it was the hidden work of women in family businesses—who tended to be white—that was most often overlooked by census enumerators. This type of underenumeration was a major cause of the racial participation gap puzzle that has eluded economists for decades.

A further avenue for research would be to develop a model of the effects of self-employment on married women's labor force participation in the current period. In addition to the increased gap in self-employment rates for white and black men since the turn of the century, we have observed a substantial increase in the propensity of white married women to become self-employed on their own account (as opposed to the connection to their husband's business that was imputed for 1880 and 1900). This increase exists even though women can expect to receive lower average annual earnings while engaged in self-employment than they would in the wage labor market.[2] This difference in the relationship between self-employment and married women's participation in the labor force is likely due to the increased flexibility afforded by self-employment (a benefit assumed to be more desirable to women than men) and requires a new perspective and modeling approach for the 1990 data.

All said, the results of this book imply that family business matters. It matters for estimating the productivity of the U.S. economy, it matters for understanding the true labor force participation of married women, and it matters for analyzing differences in the labor market experiences of black and white men and women.

NOTES

1. Goldin (1994).
2. Aronson (1991).

Bibliography

Marjorie Abel and Nancy Folbre. "A Methodology for Revising Estimates: Female Market Participation in the U.S. Before 1940." *Historical Methods* **23(4)**, Fall 1990, 167-176.

Robert Aronson. *Self-Employment: A Labor Market Perspective.* New York: ILR Press, 1991.

Gertrude Bancroft. *The American Labor Force: Its Growth and Changing Composition.* New York: John Wiley & Sons, 1958.

Durand Bell. "Why Participation Rates of Black and White Wives Differ." *Journal of Human Resources* **9**, Fall 1974, 465-79.

Ada Heather-Bigg. "The Wife's Contribution to Family Income." *Economic Journal* **4**, 1894, 51-8.

Francine D. Blau and Marianne A. Ferber. *The Economics of Women, Men, and Work.* Englewood Cliffs, N.J.: Prentice-Hall, 1986.

Alan S. Blinder. "Wage Discrimination: Reduced Form and Structural Estimates." *Journal of Human Resources* **8(4)**, 1973, 436-55.

Christine E. Bose. "Devaluing Women's Work: The Undercount of Women's Employment in 1900 and 1980," in *Hidden Aspects of Women's Work.* Christine Bose, Roslyn Feldberg, and Natalie Sokoloff, eds. New York: Praeger, 1987.

William G. Bowen and Aldrich Finegan. *The Economics of Labor Force Participation.* Princeton: Princeton University Press, 1969.

Jeanne Boydston. *Home and Work: Housework, Wages, and the Ideology of Labor in the Early Republic.* New York: Oxford University Press, 1990.

Glen G. Cain. *Married Women in the Labor Force: An Economic Analysis.* Chicago: University of Chicago Press, 1966.

Glen G. Cain. "Female Labor Supply". In *Handbook of Labor Economics*, vol. I. Orley Ashenfelter and Richard Layard, eds. New York: North-Holland, 1986.

Anne Carter. *Structural Change in the American Economy*. Cambridge, MA: Harvard University Press, 1970.

Susan B. Carter. "Comment: The Female Labor Force and American Economic Growth, 1890-1980," by Claudia Goldin, in *Long-Term Factors in American Economic Growth*. Stanley L. Engerman and Robert E. Gallman, eds. Chicago: University of Chicago Press, 1986, 594-604.

Susan B. Carter and Richard Sutch. "Fixing the Facts: Editing of the 1880 U.S. Census and Long-Term Trends in the Labor Force and the Sociology of Official Statistics." *Historical Methods* **29(1)**, Winter 1996, 1-35.

Susan B. Carter and Richard Sutch. "Self-Employment in the Age of Big Business: Toward an Appreciation of an American Labor Market Institution." *Working Papers on the History of Retirement, No. 7*. Berkeley: University of California, Berkeley, Institute of Business and Economic Research, March 1996.

Alfred D. Chandler, Jr. *Strategy and Structure: Chapters in the History of the Industrial Enterprise*. Cambridge, MA: MIT Press, 1962.

Penelope Ciancanelli. *Women's Transition to Wage Labor: A Critique of Labor Force Statistics and Re-estimation of the Labor Force Participation of Married Women in the United States, 1900-1930*. Unpublished doctoral dissertation, Department of Economics, New School for Social Research, 1983.

Margo A. Conk. "Accuracy, Efficiency, and Bias: The Interpretation of Women's Work in the U.S. Census of Occupations, 1890-1940." *Historical Methods* **14(2)**, Spring 1981, 65-72.

Patricia A. Daly. "Unpaid Family Workers: Long-Term Decline Continues." *Monthly Labor Review*, October 1982, 3-5.

D. Defoe. *Everybody's Business is Nobody's Business,* 1725.

A. Doran. *A Lady of the Last Century,* 1775.

Claude Evans Driskell. *The History of Chicago Black Dental Professionals, 1850- 1983*. Chicago: Claude E. Driskell, 1982.

Louis J. Ducoff and Gertrude Bancroft. "Experiment in the Measurement of Unpaid Family Labor in Agriculture." *Journal of the American Statistical Association* **40**, 205-213.

Richard Edwards, Michael Reich, and Thomas Weisskopf. *The Capitalist Systems*. Englewood Cliffs, NJ: Prentice-Hall, 1978.

William E. Even and David A. Macpherson. "The Decline of Private-Sector Unionism and the Gender Wage Gap." *Journal of Human Resources* **28:2**, Spring 1993, 279-296.

Robert Fairlie. *Ethnic and Racial Entrepreneurship: A Study of Historical and*

Contemporary Differences. Studies in Entrepreneurship Series, New York: Garland Publishing, 1996.

Robert Fairlie and Bruce Meyer. "Ethnic and Racial Self-Employment Differences and Possible Explanations." *Journal of Human Resources* **31:4**, 1996, 757-793.

Farmer's Wife, 1915, 18-19; 1919, 34; 1928, 22.

Nancy Folbre. "The Unproductive Housewife: Her Evolution in Nineteenth-Century Economic Thought." *Signs: Journal of Women in Culture and Society* **16(31)**, Spring 1991, 463-485.

Nancy Folbre and Marjorie Abel. "Women's Work and Women's Households: Gender Bias in the U.S. Census." *Social Research* **56(3)**, Autumn 1989, 545-569.

Martha Norby Fraundorf. "The Labor Force Participation of Turn-of-the-Century Married Women." *Journal of Economic History* **39(2)**, June 1979, 401-419.

Lisa Geib-Gundersen and Elizabeth Zahrt. "A New Look at U.S. Agricultural Productivity Growth, 1800-1910." *Journal of Economic History* **56(3)**, September 1996, 679-686.

Claudia Goldin. "Female Labor Force Participation: The Origin of Black and White Differences, 1870 and 1880." *Journal of Economic History* **37(1)**, March 1977, 87-112.

Claudia Goldin. "The Changing Economic Role of Women: A Quantitative Approach." *Journal of Interdisciplinary History* **13(4)**, Spring 1983, 707-733.

Claudia Goldin. "The Female Labor Force and American Economic Growth, 1890- 1980," in *Long-Term Factors in American Economic Growth.* Stanley L. Engerman and Robert E. Gallman, eds. Chicago: University of Chicago Press, 1986, 557-594.

Claudia Goldin. "Life-Cycle Labor-Force Participation of Married Women: Historical Evidence and Implications." *Journal of Labor Economics* **7(1)**, 1989, 20-47.

Claudia Goldin. *Understanding the Gender Gap: An Economic History of American Women.* New York: Oxford University Press, 1990.

Claudia Goldin. "The U-Shaped Female Labor Force Function in Economic Development and Economic History." NBER Working Paper No. 4707, April 1994.

David Gordon, Richard Edwards, and Michael Reich. *Segmented Work, Divided Workers.* New York: Cambridge University Press, 1982.

R. Higgs. "Racial Wage Differentials and Segregation in Competitive Labor

Markets: An Empirical Report." University of Washington, Discussion Paper No. 75-8, September 1975.

Joseph A. Hill. *Women in Gainful Occupations: 1870 to 1920.* Census Monograph IX. Washington, D.C.: U.S. Government Printing Office, 1929.

A. J. Jaffe. "Trends in the Participation of Women in the Working Force." *Monthly Labor Review* **79**, May 1956, 559-565.

Joan M. Jensen. "Cloth, Butter and Boarders: Women's Household Production for the Market." *Review of Radical Political Economics* **12(2)**, Summer 1980, 14-24.

Linda K. Kerber. "Separate Spheres, Female Worlds, Woman's Place: The Rhetoric of Women's History." *Journal of American History* **75**, 1988, 9-39.

Christine Kleinegger. "Out of the Barns and into the Kitchens: Transformations in Farm Women's Work in the First Half of the Twentieth Century," in Barbara Drygulski Wright et. al., eds., *Women, Work, and Technology: Transformations.* Ann Arbor: University of Michigan Press, 1987.

Evelyn L. Lehrer. "The Impact of Children on Married Women's Labor Supply: Black- White Differentials Revisted." *Journal of Human Resources* **27:3**, Summer 1992, 422-444.

Margaret Levenstein. "African American Entrepreneurship: The View from the 1910 Census." *Business and Economic History* **24(1)**, Fall 1995.

Julie A. Matthaei. *An Economic History of Women in America.* New York: Shocken Books, 1982.

Grant McConnell. *The Decline of Agrarian Democracy.* Berkeley: University of California Press, 1953.

Jacob Mincer. "Labor Force Participation of Married Women: A Study in Labor Supply." In National Bureau of Economic Research, *Aspects of Labor Economics*, Princeton, N.J.: NBER, 63-106.

Ronald L. Oaxaca. "Male-Female Wage Differentials in Urban Labor Markets." *International Economic Review* **9**, 1973, 693-709.

Ronald L. Oaxaca and Michael R. Ransom. "On Discrimination and the Decomposition of Wage Differentials." *Journal of Econometrics* **61**, 1994, 5-21.

Valerie Oppenheimer. *The Female Labor Force in the U.S.: Demographic and Economic Factors Governing its Growth and Changing Composition.* Berkeley: University of California, Population Monograph Series #5, 1970.

Virginia Penny. *The Employments of Women: A Cyclopadia of Woman's Work.* Boston: Walker, Wise, and Co., 1863.

A. L. Peterson. "What the Wage-Earning Woman Contributes to Family Support," *Annals of American Academy* **143**, May 1929, 74-93.

Ivy Pinchbeck. *Women Workers and the Industrial Revolution, 1750-1850.* New Jersey: Frank Cass and Co. Ltd., 1930.

Margaret G. Reid. *Economics of Household Production.* New York: John Wiley and Sons, Inc., 1934.

Elyce J. Rotella. "Women's Labor Force Participation and the Decline of the Family Economy in the United States." *Explorations in Economic History* **17**, 1980, 95-117.

Robert W. Smuts. *Women and Work in America.* New York: Columbia University Press, 1959.

Robert W. Smuts. "The Female Labor Force: A Case Study in the Interpretation of Historical Statistics." *Journal of the American Statistical Association* **55**, March 1960, 71-79.

James A. Sweet. *Women in the Labor Force.* New York: Seminar Press, 1973.

Louise A. Tilly and Joan W. Scott. *Women, Work, and Family.* New York: Routledge, 1978.

Rolla Milton Tyron. *Household Manufacturers in the United States, 1640-1860.* Chicago: University of Chicago Press, 1917.

U.S. Census Office, Department of the Interior. "Statistics of the Population of the United States." Washington, D.C.: U.S. Government Printing Office, 1880 through 1990.

Francis Amasa Walker. *Political Economy.* New York: Henry Holt, 1883.

Harold D. Woodman. "Comment: Female Labor Force Participation: The Origin of Black and White Differences, 1870 and 1880," by Claudia Goldin. *Journal of Economic History* **37(1)**, March 1977, 109-12.

Gavin Wright. "*Understanding the Gender Gap*: A Review Article." *Journal of Economic Literature* **29(3)**, September 1991, 1153-63.

Index